EDITOR: MARTIN WINDROW

ELITE

OSPREY
MILITARY

THE TEXAS

Text by
Dr STEPHEN HARDIN
Colour plates by
RICHARD HOOK

First published in Great Britain in 1991 by
Osprey Publishing, Elms Court, Chapel Way, Botley,
Oxford OX2 9LP, United Kingdom.
Email: info@ospreypublishing.com

British Library Cataloguing in Publication Data
Hardin, Stephen
   The Texas Rangers. — (Elite)
   I. Title   II. Series
   363.209764
   ISBN 1855321556

Filmset in Great Britain
Printed in China through World Print Ltd.

Artist's Note

Readers may care to note that the original paintings
from which the colour plates in this book were
prepared are available for private sale. All
reproduction copyright whatsoever is retained by the
Publishers. All enquiries should be addressed to:

   Scorpio Gallery
   P.O. Box 475,
   Hailsham,
   E. Sussex BN27 2SL

The Publishers regret that they can enter into no
correspondence upon this matter.

FOR A CATALOGUE OF ALL BOOKS PUBLISHED BY
OSPREY MILITARY AND AVIATION PLEASE WRITE TO:

The Marketing Manager, Osprey Direct USA,
PO Box 130, Sterling Heights, MI 48311-0130, USA.
Email: info@ospreydirectusa.com

The Marketing Manager, Osprey Direct UK,
PO Box 140, Wellingborough, Northants, NN8 4ZA,
United Kingdom.
Email: info@ospreydirect.co.uk

VISIT OSPREY AT
www.ospreypublishing.com

Dedication: To Samuel Hamilton Walker Hardin, a
young Texan who bears well the heavy burden and
proud legacy of his ranger name.

Acknowledgements:

During the preparation of this book the author has
incurred debts that he can never adequately repay.
The following friends and colleagues deserve special
mention: Judge Wade Anderson and Robert Bethea,
both of Austin, for badgering me into accepting the
project in the first place; Richard Scollins of Ilkeston,
Derbyshire, for frequent letters of encouragement; Dr.
Robert T. Maberry at Texas Christian University in
Fort Worth, Dr. Vista K. McCroskey at Southwest
Texas State University in San Marcos, Thomas Ricks
Lindley of Austin, Oscar Barrera and James F. Green
of San Marcos, and Kevin R. Young of San Antonio
for reading portions of the manuscript; Ralph Elder,
John Slate, and the entire staff at the Barker Texas
History Center, University of Texas at Austin;
Michael R. Green, John Anderson, Donaly E. Brice
and the staff of the Archives Division, Texas State
Library; Sharon Crutchfield and Berniece Strong,
both formerly at The Daughters of the Republic of
Texas Library at the Alamo, San Antonio; Mike Cox,
Department of Public Safety, Austin; Tom Burks at
the Texas Ranger Museum in Waco; Elaine Brown
Sullivan at the Texas Memorial Museum, University
of Texas at Austin. Thanks also to Robert M. Bell of
Austin for photographic counsel. For his singular
insight, thanks to Captain Jack Dean, Texas Rangers,
San Antonio. Finally, profound gratitude to Deborah
for suffering through yet another campaign.

Author's note:

The old-time Texas Rangers were far handier with
Colt revolvers and Bowie knives than dictionaries and
style manuals. The standard [sic] after every
misspelling and grammatical error would have
cluttered the text to little advantage. Throughout,
therefore, quotations are rendered as originally written.

THE TEXAS RANGERS

THE EARLY YEARS, 1823–1839

During the first two decades of the 19th century the province of Texas frustrated the harried officials of New Spain. The vastness of the region made it difficult to establish a cordon of forts, and the mounted Plains Indians raided almost at will. The worst of these were the Comanches, the 'Lords of the South Plains'—the appellation was deserved. Demonstrating astonishing horsemanship, Comanches swept down from their camps west of the Balcones Escarpment to steal mounts, kill men, and kidnap women and children. Emboldened by their successes in Texas, Comanches had begun to raid far into the Mexican interior.

In 1821 Mexicans achieved their independence from Spain, but changing governments in Mexico City made little difference to life in Texas. There Indians continued to make life for the thinly spread Hispanic settlers of Texas—*tejanos*—a constant gamble. Mexican officials realized that they first had to populate Texas if they were to combat the Indian threat. Few Mexicans, however, could be induced to move to a region generally regarded as the *despoblado*, the unoccupied land.

Moses Austin, a former Spanish subject in upper Louisiana, proposed what appeared to be a workable solution: colonizing the area with Americans who would become Spanish citizens. In 1821 officials approved a grant permitting him to distribute 20,000 acres among 300 families. Austin's death coincided with the end of Spanish rule, but Stephen F. Austin continued his father's work. Soon other American *empresarios* founded additional colonies along the fertile banks of the Brazos River and in the pine forest of East Texas.

At first the union was a productive one. *Tejanos* were happy to gain allies in their war against marauding Indians. For their part the American

Stephen F. Austin; engraving by Charles K. Burt, c.1824. (Texas Memorial Museum, Austin, Texas)

immigrants, 90 per cent of whom came from Southern states, were grateful for free land, no taxes, a liberal constitution modelled after their own, and a dispensation to retain their slaves even though Mexico had already abolished the practice. The fiercely independent Southerners, however, had no intention of melting into Mexican society. Proud products of Jacksonian Democracy, these sturdy 'crackers' were ruthless in their ambition, cocksure that they were any man's equal, and eager to fight if that supposition were questioned.

Southerners brought the trappings of their culture with them, not the least important of which was a

3

ranger tradition. During the 1600s the term ranger had been used in Scotland to describe armed men who 'ranged' a tract of countryside against the raids of enemy clans. The practice migrated to the American colonies where as early as 1739 James Oglethorpe raised a Georgia unit called the Troop of Highland Rangers. After the Jacobite defeat at Culloden in 1746 thousands of Scots emigrated to North America, and many settled in Southern states where Celtic folkways had already taken root. Later the name ranger was applied to the gunmen whom the settlers hired to patrol the woods against Indians and white criminals. In times of crisis the militiamen would muster, but more often than not they would look to the local ranger to organize and lead them — he was the professional.

When Anglo-Celtic immigrants first settled in Texas the Karankawas and Tonkawas proved more of a nuisance than the horse-borne Plains Indians. 'Kronks' and 'Tonks', as American settlers came to call them, were more often petty thieves than deadly warriors. Even so, as early as 1823 *empresario* Stephen F. Austin employed ten men to act as rangers and apparently paid them out of his own pocket. Later Austin led a 20-man expedition against a band of Tonkawas who had stolen horses. When Austin's rangers overtook the raiding party they retrieved the

horses, lashed the braves, and admonished the chief that future horse thieves would be summarily shot.

In 1826 a band of Tawakonis infiltrated Austin's colony in pursuit of their traditional tribal enemies, the Tonkawas. They did not hesitate, however, to acquire American horses when the opportunity arose. James J. Ross, leading 31 militiamen, attacked 16 Indians, killing eight and wounding five. In the face of a growing Indian menace Austin planned a campaign against the Tawakonis and their equally war-like neighbours the Wacos. He advocated employing the friendly Cherokees, Shawnees, and Delawares as allies; but the Mexican commandant, mistrustful of such an alliance, forbade it. Austin and his settlers were ordered to delay any punitive campaign until regular army troops could be summoned from the interior.

While the Mexican commandant worked through official channels, Indians continued to steal horses and occasionally to kill settlers. Austin responded in a typically American manner; he called a conference of the representatives of the six militia districts to devise a system of defence, and together they elected to keep a permanent force of 20 to 30 rangers. According to the agreement each landowner was to serve or provide a substitute for one month for every half-league of land that he owned. Records do not reveal, however, whether this force ever became operational.

From the beginning the rangers were irregulars. Each man was expected to be well mounted and well armed from his own resources. Openly disdainful of military discipline, these wilful volunteers would have been offended had they been mistaken for regulars. This was unlikely: rangers fought under no flag, wore no uniform, and in practice observed no prescribed length of service. One would even have to stretch the definition of the term to call them militia, for militia mustered at regular intervals for drill. Except for the paid captains the troopers responded only in times of crisis, and took their leave the instant they deemed the threat to be over.

The first organized companies
The organization was formalized to some degree

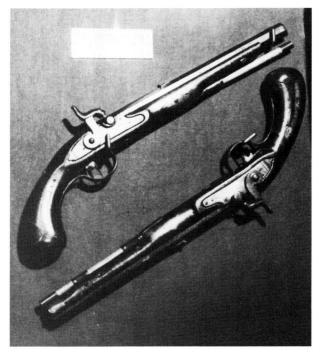

Stephen F. Austin's flintlock pistols. These are typical of those used by Texas Rangers during the

Mexican Republic period. (Texas Memorial Museum, Austin, Texas)

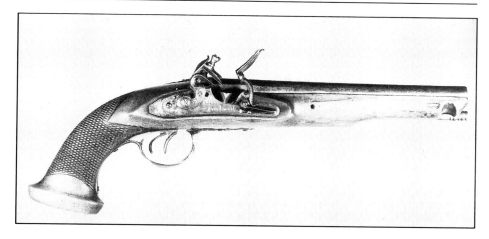

The brass buttplate on this double-barrelled flintlock pistol identifies it as having belonged to a member of 'Ranging Company, number 3' from San Felipe de Austin. (Author's collection, courtesy Douglas Kubicek)

during the Texas Revolution of 1835–1836. The causes of the revolt need not be detailed here, but it is noteworthy that American colonists—'Texian' was the term they now preferred—were too independent, headstrong, and contemptuous of the centralist policies of dictator Antonio López de Santa Anna to live amicably under Mexican rule. (For a closer examination see Philip Haythornthwaite, *The Alamo and the Texas War for Independence*, Osprey MAA 173.)

On 24 November 1835 the interim Texas government approved an ordinance providing for a corps of mounted gunmen. This unit was to be better organized than the makeshift posses that had gone before. On that date the general council, the interim rebel government, established a corps of Texas Rangers. It authorized three companies of 56 men, each to be headed by a captain aided by first and second lieutenants. A major would direct the operations of the companies and would report directly to the commander-in-chief. Gone were the informal enlistments of the past: privates signed on for one full year

and would earn $1.25 per day for 'pay, rations, clothing, and horse service'. It was stipulated that each ranger was to stand ready with a good horse, saddle, bridle, and blanket, as well as 100 rounds of powder and ball.

On the night of 28 November Isaac W. Burton, William H. Arrinton, and John J. Tumlinson were elected to captain the new companies. Delegates nominated R. M. Williamson and James Kerr for major; Williamson, a Georgia native and prominent attorney, won the post.

Despite appearances, Robert McAlpin Williamson was a fortunate choice. At the age of 15 polio confined him to his bed for two years and caused his right leg to permanently bend at the knee. The wooden leg that he wore from the knee to the ground resulted in his nickname 'Three-Legged Willie'. The young man was determined that his affliction would not prevent him from leading an active life. He studied law during his illness and was admitted to the Georgia bar at the age of nineteen. In 1826 he migrated to Texas, where his firebrand editorials against the Mexican government earned him a reputation as the 'Patrick Henry of the Texas Revolution'. They also caused the Mexican politicians he denounced to place a bounty on his head. If Williamson's opinions won him the enmity of Mexican centralists, Texians grew to respect him, naming him a district judge. Hearty frontiersmen admired the way he refused to let his disability hinder him. He had an eye for the ladies, played the banjo, and—seemingly unaware of his peg leg—danced a devilish jig.

Texian officials raised the ranging companies to combat the Indian menace, but as Mexican battalions

Major Robert McAlpin Williamson—'Three-legged Willie', who commanded the first organized, paid ranger force from November 1835. (Prints and Photographs Collection, Barker Texas History Center, University of Texas at Austin)

swept across Texas rangers were often the only men organized and ready to fight them. Captain George Kimball's Gonzales Ranging Company of Mounted Volunteers, for example, were the only Texians to assist the besieged Alamo defenders, and shared their fate. After the defeats at the Alamo and Goliad, Gen. Sam Houston ordered Maj. Williamson to muster his rangers along the Old San Antonio Road near Bastrop to serve as a fighting rearguard and to observe enemy troop movements. Small ranger contingents lingered behind as most American colonists joined the hysterical exodus that came to be known as the 'Runaway Scrape'.

In March 1836 a woman, dazed, exhausted, and almost naked, stumbled into Capt. John Tumlinson's camp on the Colorado River. The woman, a Mrs. Hibbons, related how a Comanche war party had

ambushed her family; her husband and brother had been murdered and she, along with her young son and an infant, had been captured. While in captivity she heard a loud booming in the distance toward Béxar, but only later did she learn that the din was Santa Anna's artillery hammering the walls of the Alamo. Her ordeal, however, had only just begun. The baby's crying so annoyed one of the warriors that he wrested the child from Mrs. Hibbons's arms and, before the horrified mother's eyes, smashed its head against the nearest tree. Later, scornful of a white woman's ability to escape in such rough terrain, the braves neglected to guard the bereaved mother. They misjudged Mrs. Hibbons: she fled under the cover of darkness, and after days in the wilderness stumbled on the ranger camp, where she begged the men to rescue the young son she had abandoned.

This was just the sort of job the rangers were paid to do. Tumlinson's men retraced Mrs. Hibbons's trail. Early the next morning they located the Comanche camp while the complacent raiders, never dreaming that Texians could overtake them, snoozed in their buffalo robes. Tumlinson led a headlong charge into the camp. The rangers reached the white boy before the Indians could cut his throat. One raider was shot down in the mêlée, but the rest escaped into the brush. A grateful Mrs. Hibbons was reunited with her child. During the mission to recover the Hibbons boy the rangers had demonstrated courage and determination, but they had also been lucky: lucky that Mrs. Hibbons had located their camp; lucky that they picked up the Indians' trail so quickly; lucky that they had caught the Comanches off guard.

On 21 April 1836, victory at San Jacinto secured a respite for the struggling Republic of Texas. Texians had managed to defeat Santa Anna, but elsewhere they were not doing as well. As Anglo-Celtic settlers migrated westward they began to encroach on the *Comanchería*, the upland country west of the Balcones Escarpment which the Comanches considered their domain. Naturally, hostile contacts became more frequent. The ranging companies could not hope to patrol such a vast frontier, and war parties penetrated the frontier at will.

In May 1839 Capt. John Bird and 35 rangers located 27 Indians, whom they pursued. Following the fleeing braves the rangers, falling for an old

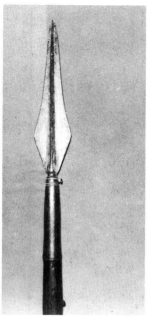

An English view of a Texas ranging company. Note the presence of the tejano *ranger riding alongside his*

*Anglo-American comrades. (*Illustrated London News, *1842)*

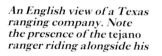

Early Texas Rangers feared Mexican lances more than any other weapon; this specimen suggests why. (Daughters of the Republic of Texas Library at the Alamo, San Antonio)

Comanche trick, were soon surrounded by about 240 warriors who had been concealed for that purpose. The Texians dismounted to make a stand in a ravine, where they kept the tribesmen at bay with their rifles. Had the Indians been willing to accept the losses it would have required they could easily have wiped out the ranging force. Instead they withdrew after killing seven Texians, including Capt. Bird. Having accomplished nothing, the humiliated Texians limped back to the settlements.

Throughout the late 1830s the raids increased. Both sides became aware that this was not merely a fight over hunting grounds or stolen horses. Tales of Comanche cruelty abounded. To the Texians the Comanche represented nothing more than a 'squalid savage' whose presence prevented the spread of civilization. In response they matched, at times even surpassed, Indian atrocities. The conflict became a brutal race war, a clash of vastly incongruous world views, as the events of 1840 would amply demonstrate—events in which the rangers would play a leading role.

BATTLES OF THE REPUBLIC, 1840–1845

Texians envisioned their infant republic stretching westward to the Pacific, but old enemies were constant impediments to dreams of empire. On the western frontier, which extended only to the Balcones Escarpment, the Comanches presented a seemingly insurmountable barrier to western migration. Conditions were only slightly better along the southern border. Mexican officials had never recognized Texian independence and considered all land above the Nueces River a stolen province that would someday be reconquered. Until that day came, however, they would harry the upstart rebels with border raids.

Making matters worse, the republic was bankrupt. It boasted a small regular army, but this was

John Coffee Hays, the legendary 'Captain Jack' who introduced Colt revolvers. (Prints and

Photographs Collection, Barker Texas History Center, University of Texas at Austin)

expensive to uniform, arm, and deploy. To face Comanches and Mexican *rancheros* on equal terms required blooded horses, which were also high-dollar items. Texas leaders faced a pitiless cycle: settlers demanded defence; defence cost money; money was non-existent. The exigency of the moment required an inexpensive para-military force that would supply its own weapons and mounts, provide for itself in the field, and require no uniform: in short, Texas Rangers.

Ranger service attracted a certain type of frontiersman. In the main they were young single men, for those with families could not afford to spend months on campaign. Independent and practical, rangers had no patience with the 'spit and polish' foolishness of the regular army. 'Discipline, in the common acceptation of the term', one of them explained, 'was not regarded as absolutely essential.' A distinct form of frontier leadership emerged. A ranger captain was selected by men who trusted his judgement and

recognized his ability. He attracted volunteers by force of personality and reputation. Events were unfolding that would provide captains with ample opportunity to make their names.

On 19 March 1840 after a year of almost constant warfare, a delegation of some 65 Comanches rode into San Antonio to negotiate a peace treaty. Texian commissioners had agreed to the meeting on the condition that Indians release all white captives; but Chief Muguara, the head of the Comanche delegation, had brought only two, a small Mexican boy and teenager Matilda Lockhart. The girl's appearance did not improve the Texians' mood. Matilda tearfully admitted that she had been 'utterly degraded'. One of the women who attended her described how 'her head, arms and face were full of bruises, and sores, and her nose actually burnt off to the bone—all the fleshy end gone, and a great scab formed on the end of the bone. Both nostrils were wide open and denuded of flesh'. Matilda also reported that, in violation of the agreement, the Indians held more captives back in their camps. When the two parties met in the Council House, a local meeting hall, the Texian delegation informed Muguara that until all white captives were returned he and the entire Comanche contingent would be retained as hostages. Predictably, the braves grabbed their weapons and a general mêlée ensued. Eight whites and 35 Indians, including Muguara, were killed.

The Comanches swore vengeance. They were so inflamed by what they interpreted as Texian treachery that they reportedly slaughtered about 13 white captives. The greatest blunder in the history of Texas-Indian relations, the Council House Fight thwarted peaceful contacts between the Comanche nation and the Republic of Texas, and guaranteed that rangers would be gainfully employed for several years to come.

Through the spring and summer of 1840 the loose confederacy of Southern Comanche gathered deep within the *Comanchería* to plan the greatest raid in the tribe's history. The blow fell early in August, when a contingent numbering close to a thousand swept down from the high plains into the areas of white settlement. The marauders by-passed San Antonio and drove towards the coast, falling on the unsuspecting town of Victoria where they killed 15 Texians and ran off nearly 2,000 horses. On 8 August the raiders arrived in Linnville, a small port town on Lavaca Bay. Most of the terrified residents escaped in rowing boats. Hovering off shore just beyond arrow range, they watched helplessly as the Indians frolicked in the surf, killed cattle, sacked warehouses, and—after they had seized all they could carry—burned the town.

By the time the Comanches had reached Linnville the rangers had mustered. Companies under John Tumlinson, Ben McCulloch, and Matthew 'Old Paint' Caldwell observed the movements of the Indian formation. Rangers could never hope to confront such numbers directly, so they harried the Comanches in a series of hit-and-run attacks. At the same time they despatched riders to Gen. Felix Huston in command of the regular army, with information regarding the Indians' line of escape. Rangers slowed the Comanches while the main army positioned men to cut them off. They were aided in this by the Indians themselves. Loaded down with booty and hindered by the enormous horse herd, the Comanches inched their way towards the

Texas terrain map. (Erwin Raisz, Landforms of the United States, sixth revised ed., 1957)

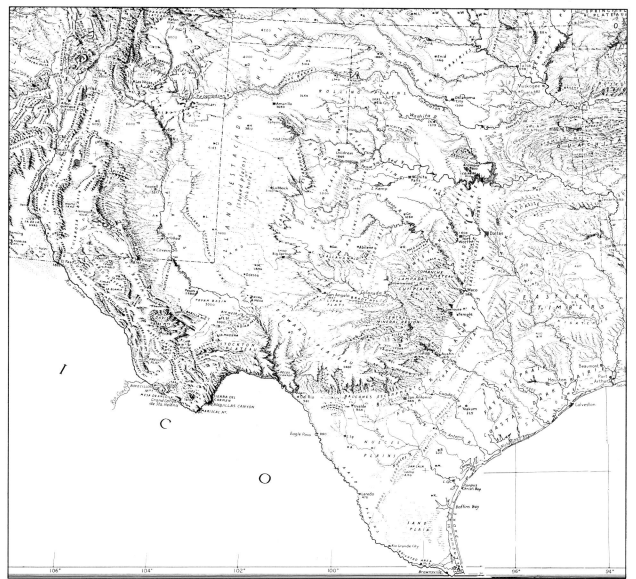

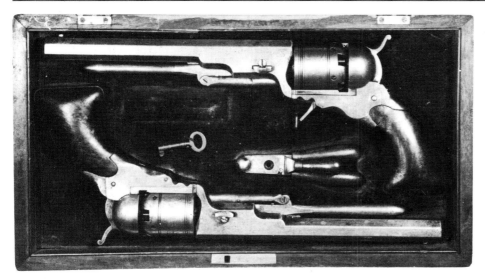

Comanchería. Repeatedly the rangers bore in, killed two or three braves, and darted away before the loot-laden Indians could retaliate. The mounted Texians, in an ironic role reversal, fought like Indians, while the Comanches, slowed by their impedimenta, plodded along like white regulars.

Meanwhile some 200 Texians assembled at Plum Creek, south-east of Austin, to intercept the Comanche withdrawal. Gen. Huston led a mix of rangers, regulars, local militia, Tonkawa allies, and independent frontiersmen anxious for any opportunity to kill Comanches. As the Indians approached on 12 August Texians were awed by their regalia. The outrageous garb of one warrior attracted the special attention of Reverend Z. N. Morrell: 'He was riding a very fine horse, held in by a fine American bridle, with a red ribbon eight or ten feet long tied to the tail of the horse. He was dressed in elegant style, from the goods stolen at Linnville, with a high-top silk hat, fine pair of boots and leather gloves, an elegant broadcloth coat, hind part before, with brass buttons shining brightly right up and down his back. When he first made his appearance he was carrying a large umbrella stretched.'

Led by the rangers, the Texas cavalry charged the Comanche flank. The horse herd stampeded, the Indians scattered, and the Texians pursued. With braves fleeing in all directions, Gen. Huston watched what he had hoped would be a crushing final battle degenerate into a running fight. Even so, by sundown the bodies of 80 warriors were littered over 30 miles of prairie; the Texians lost one man. Rummaging through jettisoned Indian plunder, rangers discovered a number of baby alligators—the braves had wanted proof that they had raided all the way to the coast.

Based on the casualty ratio, the Texians claimed victory; but that only reflected their European perspective. Comanches normally avoided pitched battles and the high losses they inevitably produced, relying instead on stealthy tactics. True, many warriors had been lost, but many more had escaped. Still, Plum Creek was decisive in one sense. Never again did a large body of Comanches drive into areas of Texian settlement. Instead, small war parties reverted to the old hit-and-run raids, of which they were the acknowledged masters.

In the autumn of 1840, eager to maintain the momentum achieved at Plum Creek, Col. John Moore led a company up the Colorado River 'half way to Sante Fé', where he hit the Comanches in one of their home camps. The surprise was total; the rangers indiscriminately shot down more than a hundred Comanches. 'The bodies of men, women, and children were to be seen on every hand wounded, dying, and dead', Moore boasted.

Captain Jack and the Colt
Comanche supremacy was waning at the time when a young ranger captain was rising to prominence; his name was John Coffee Hays. The 21-year-old Hays rode into San Antonio in around 1837. A surveyor by

Samuel H. Walker, the great Mexican War scout, as the eastern press imagined he must have looked. (Brother Jonathan's Almanac, Philadelphia, 1847)

The real Samuel H. Walker, contrasting with the romantic image; there is little here that reveals the bold daring which inspired his followers to call him 'Mad Walker'. (Library of Congress, Washington, DC)

trade, 'Jack' was a quiet, modest young man whom the local citizens esteemed as 'a popular man and a good Indian fighter'. He seemed to have received his early training under Erastus 'Deaf' Smith and Henry W. Karnes, both heroes of the Texas Revolution. In 1838 he joined a band of friendly Delawares during their ambush of a Comanche war-party and carefully noted the Indian tactics of stealth and surprise. After a brief apprenticeship Hays's natural leadership asserted itself.

Like Maj. Williamson, Hays did not fit the stereotype of the rugged pioneer fighter. He was short and slight of build, and his boyish face made him appear younger than he was; only his cold eyes and steady self-confidence bespoke authority. Men who served under him testified that he was fearless. The comment of Chief Flacco, a Lipan ally who rode with

Hays against the Comanches on numerous occasions, is perhaps the most expressive: 'Captain Jack heap brave; not afraid to go to hell by himself.'

In addition to being 'heap brave', Hays also identified a basic tactical problem. In the forest frontiersmen had relied on their Kentucky long rifles, but on the Texas plains they were hopelessly outclassed; the very length that made the rifles so accurate rendered them impossibly cumbersome for men on horseback. Once a ranger had discharged the long arm he was forced to dismount to reload. Rate of fire was an additional worry. As Ranger Noah Smithwick explained: 'Primitive as the Indians' weapons were, they gave them an advantage over the old single-barreled, muzzle-loading rifle in the matter of rapid shooting, an advantage which told heavily in a charge. An Indian could discharge a dozen

Period engraving of Ben McCulloch, who scouted for Zachary Taylor before Buena Vista. (Prints and

Photographs Collection, Barker Texas History Center, University of Texas at Austin)

the Indians bore in for the kill. Hays then played his ace, ordering his men to mount and counter-charge with the Colt five-shooter. 'Powder-burn them!' Hays shouted as his men rode among the Comanches. No one ever doubted the courage of Comanche braves, but they had never seen a pistol that could fire without reloading. Clearly, this was bad medicine: the Indians broke and fled. The rangers pursued for over three miles, killing the full distance. By the time the Texians reined in 30 of their enemies lay dead on the prairie. The Comanches knew who had led the rangers that day. 'I will never again fight Jack Hays', one war chief declared. How could he expect his warriors to fight men who had 'a shot for every finger of the hand'?

The captain insisted that his men be accurate marksmen. Ranger Jim Nichols described how Hays 'put up a post about the size of a common man, then put up another about 40 yards farther on. We would run our horses full speed and discharge our rifles at the first post, draw our pistles and fire at the second.' Nichols admitted that at first there was some 'wild shooting', but within two months 'thare was not many men that would not put his balls in the center of the posts.'

It was not enough simply to be a good shot. Nichols explained how the rangers would also 'try rideing like Comanche Indians': 'After practisng for three or four months we became so purfect that we would run our horses half or full speede and pick up a hat, a coat, a blanket, or rope, or even a silver dollar, stand up in the saddle, throw ourselves on the side of our horses with only a foot and a hand to be seen, and then shoot our pistols under the horses neck, rise up and reverse, etc.'

Hays taught the rangers how to defeat the Indians. The process would take almost four decades to complete, but the introduction of the Colt revolver marked the beginning of the end for the Comanche nation. Beyond that point Texas Rangers were the 'Lords of the South Plains'. Packing his Colt revolver, the ranger could best both the Indian's lance and the Mexican's lasso.

Capt. Hays came to rely heavily upon his Colts. While surveying the hill country west of Austin with a group of rangers in the fall of 1841 he was cut off by more than a hundred Comanches. He retired to the summit of Enchanted Rock, a bald, oval-shaped

arrows while a man was loading a gun, and if they could manage to draw our fire at once they had us at their mercy unless we had a safe retreat.'

Hays recognized the potential of Samuel Colt's revolver as the key to Indian warfare. The Texas Navy had purchased Colt Patterson pistols for its sailors, and by 1844 Hays had procured them. During the summer of that year the five-shot revolver made its combat debut along the Pedernales River northwest of San Antonio. Hays and 14 rangers were ambushed by more than 70 Comanches. Hays had his men dismount to fire their long rifles. As the Indians galloped within range, the rangers unleashed a volley. Knowing it would take time for the Texians to reload,

granite mountain, and took up a defensive position. Hays, armed with a long rifle and two Patterson revolvers, held the Comanches at bay for several hours. Just as Hays was down to his last round his rangers rescued him. Because of that action and others Colt's revolver became an indelible component of the Texas myth.

The Texians were transformed by the Colt revolver, but even more so by the land for which they fought. The natives had given them new perspectives on mounted warfare and they embraced those elements they found useful. From the *tejano* they adopted the bandanna, Spanish saddle, spike-rowelled spurs, Mexican blankets, gourd canteens, and *pinole*, a crushed corn mixture that could be munched on the trail. From the Comanche they adopted tracking, fieldcraft, and hit-and-run tactics.

This process of cultural borrowing created a new type of light horseman. Americans had used cavalry before, but these irregulars bore little resemblance to the US Dragoons with their bright sabres and blue uniforms. Although recruit John Forester had 'seen a good deal of the primitive ways of Texas', he was nonetheless astonished by the rangers' appearance and habits:

'The men were, in physical make-up, as fine a body of men as I ever saw, but the uniform was altogether new, unique and picturesque. Most of them were

dressed in skins, some wearing parts of buffalo robes, deer skins and bear skins, and some entirely naked to the waist, but having heavy leggings and necessary breech-clouts. All were well armed and well mounted. I understood, and learned for a certainty afterward, that they subsisted mostly on buffalo meat and venison, rarely ever using bread, and still more rarely ever getting any coffee.'

On 29 December 1845 Texas was annexed to the United States, an act which led to war with Mexico. Texas Rangers quickly joined Gen. Zachary Taylor's American army to settle old scores.

LOS DIABLOS TEJANOS, 1846–1848

US regulars regarded the enemy with a professional detachment; they were slow to fathom the rangers' bitter hatred for Mexicans. The explanation could be traced to the Texas Revolution and the slaughters at the Alamo and Goliad. The subsequent border clashes during the Republic period did nothing to soothe old animosities.

In the 1841 Santa Fé Expedition, an ill-conceived venture to establish Texas jurisdiction over New Mexico, the entire Texian contingent had stumbled starving into the region where they had been immediately arrested by Mexican authorities and marched to Mexico City in chains. The unfortunate members of the Sante Fé Expedition were released after much diplomatic haggling, but by then many had died in the fetid Peroté Prison.

The 1842 Mier Expedition proved an even greater disaster. Seeking revenge for Gen. Adrian Woll's brief occupation of San Antonio earlier that year, a Texian force marched on Mexico. Many sought revenge for the so-called Dawson Massacre, an incident during Woll's invasion in which Nicholas M. Dawson's company had been surrounded and

This period woodcut depicts rangers engaged in house-to-house fighting during the siege of *Monterrey, 1846* (Rough and Ready Almanac, *Philadelphia, 1848*)

virtually wiped out. (Rangers under Ben McCulloch had discovered large bodies of enemy troops massing south of the Río Grande and advised against crossing. When headstrong volunteers insisted on driving forward against all odds, McCulloch and his men had prudently abandoned the expedition.)

Instead of avenging Dawson's men, the Mier Expedition Texians quickly found themselves in a similar predicament. They fought gallantly, but outnumbered almost ten-to-one the small contingent was finally forced to surrender. The Mier prisoners were marched into the interior of Mexico, but near Salado Ewen Cameron, a feisty Scotsman and ranger captain, led an escape attempt. Mexican soldiers quickly rounded up all but a few. As punishment the 176 recaptured Texians were decimated. Mexican guards placed 159 white beans in a large earthenware jar along with 17 black ones. The prisoners were forced to reach in and pick a bean; and the Mexicans shot those who picked a black bean.

Cameron drew a white bean, but when Santa Anna learned that the ringleader of the breakout had been spared he angrily ordered his immediate execution. When the firing squad commander offered him a

Texas Ranger, 1847: this watercolour by military illustrator Joseph Hefter depicts a ranger of the Mexican–American War. His equipment exhibits much cultural borrowing from his tejano neighbours. Note the pervasive use of the lone star insignia on hat and pistols. (Author's collection)

CHARGING THROUGH THE GUERRILLA CAMP —*Page* 344.

Popular illustrations such as this one from S. Comton Smith's Chile Con Carne; or, the Camp and the Field *(1857) helped promote the rangers' fearsome reputation. (Archives Division, Texas State Archives, Austin)*

blindfold Cameron refused, declaring: 'Ewen Cameron can now, as he has often done for the liberty of Texas, look death in the face without winking.' He then tore open his hunting smock, offering his naked breast as the target, and shouted the command to fire. Mourning their fallen leader, the survivors of the lethal lottery were herded to Peroté Prison where several were killed by Mexican guards or died from disease, starvation, or exposure.

Many of the rangers now serving under Taylor had been Mier prisoners. For those like William 'Bigfoot' Wallace, Samuel H. Walker, and John McMullen the declaration of war was a *carte blanche* to exact personal revenge for slaughtered comrades. Their sentiments were expressed in the 'Ranger's Song': *Spur! spur in the chase, dash on to the fight—Cry vengeance for Texas! and God speed the right.*

When Taylor arrived at the mouth of the Nueces River in July 1845 he called for Texas volunteers. Men from that state—following annexation, 'Texan' became the accepted term—responded in droves. Jack Hays, now a colonel, commanded the First Regiment of Mounted Volunteers; George T. Wood led the Second Regiment of Mounted Volunteers, consisting of men primarily from East Texas. Neither unit was officially designated as 'Texas Rangers', but both were widely regarded as such. (Throughout the 1840s rangers were difficult to trace as such: still informal in their organization, they were raised under a variety of names. At various times they mustered as 'mounted gunmen', 'mounted volunteers', 'mounted riflemen', 'militia', and 'spies'.)

Taylor was unfamiliar with the disputed territory between the Nueces River and the Río Grande and called on Hays to provide scouts. The first of these to gain fame was Samuel Hamilton Walker. Born in Maryland and a veteran of the Indian wars in Georgia and Florida, he came to Texas in 1836 and soon 'distinguished himself for courage and coolness' serving under Hays. Taylor employed Capt. Walker when Mexican troops crossed the Río Grande and surrounded the tiny US garrison under Major Jacob Brown at Fort Texas, a makeshift post across the river from Matamoros. Taylor was determined not to have another Alamo on his hands, but he needed reliable intelligence to know how to proceed. Walker provided it. After a survey of the enemy camp he brought Taylor a careful estimate of Mexican strength. The American general now had to know conditions inside the beleaguered Fort Texas; again he called on Walker. Accompanied by six rangers, Walker made his way through the enemy cordon to inform Maj. Brown that help was on the way. The rangers then cut their way out to relay Brown's assurance to his general that the fort would hold until help arrived.

These exploits brought Walker and the Texans to national attention. The Mexican–American War was among the first in which newspaper correspondents routinely relayed their reports back home, and

This Frederic Remington engraving depicts rangers in defensive action against Mexican partisans. The charro attire is pure fancy. (Harper's Magazine, *1896)*

John Salmon 'Rip' Ford, who defeated Iron Jacket's Comanches on the Canadian River in 1858.

(Prints and Photographs Collection, Barker Texas History Center, University of Texas at Austin)

Americans could follow the various actions mere weeks after they occurred. These outlandish warriors provided good copy for many a reporter hungry for sensational stories, and readers were captivated by the romantic-sounding Texas Rangers. Hays and his men were daring, but the publicity enhanced their exotic reputation.

Monterrey and Buena Vista

Beginning with back-to-back battles at Palo Alto and Resaca de la Palma on 8 and 9 May 1846, rangers participated in almost every phase of Taylor's north-

Over the years the popular image of the Texas Ranger attired in a wild assortment of buckskins became a cliché; even so, many did affect such garments. Dating from

1839, this example would have been typical. (Prints and Photographs Collection, Barker Texas History Center, University of Texas at Austin)

ern campaign. In August of that year they served as scouts as Taylor marched his army southward into Mexico. During this advance they also rode against enemy guerrillas who harried Taylor's supply lines. It was also during this drive, while exacting 'vengeance for Texas', that rangers became notorious as 'los Diablos Tejanos'—the Texan Devils. They once apprehended a Mexican attempting to steal their horses and left his bullet-riddled corpse unburied as a reminder to other would-be horse thieves.

In mid-September the American army approached the fortified city of Monterrey, and Taylor

sent the Texans forward to secure intelligence regarding the enemy works. They grasped the opportunity to dazzle not only the enemy but also their American comrades. Luther Giddings, an officer of the 1st Ohio Volunteers, described how 'those fearless horsemen, in a spirit of boastful rivalry, vied with each other in approaching the very edge of danger. Riding singly and rapidly', Giddings recounted, 'they swept around the plain under the walls, each one in a wider and more perilous circle than his predecessor. Their proximity occasionally provoked the enemy's fire, but the Mexicans might as well have attempted to bring down skimming swallows as those racing dare-devils.'

On 20 September the rangers dismounted to serve as assault troops during the storming of Monterrey. Alongside the regular infantry Hays's men pushed into the city, knocking through adobe walls with crowbars and picking off enemy soldiers with their rifles. The fighting was house-to-house, at places hand-to-hand. At one point Taylor ordered the rangers to pull back so that his guns could bombard that section of the city. Offended, the Texans replied that they had won most of the city by themselves, and refused to retreat a single inch. With the insubordinate Texans still in position, Taylor ordered the shelling to proceed as scheduled; amazingly, none of them were hit. On 24 September Mexican Gen. Pedro de Ampudia, commanding the Monterrey garrison, asked for terms. 'Had it not been for [the rangers'] unerring rifles, there is no doubt we would have been whipped', one US volunteer admitted. Even regulars expressed a grudging respect for their dogged assault.

Shortly after the surrender of Monterrey the enlistments of many rangers ran out. With no Mexicans to fight and chafing under regular army restraints, they turned their mounts towards the Río Grande. Gen. Taylor was not altogether sorry to see them go. Even 'Old Rough and Ready' had been appalled by their 'extensive depredations and outrages' on Mexican civilians, a view shared by another regular officer:

'The departure of the Rangers would have caused more regret than was generally felt, had it not been for the lawless and vindictive spirit some of them had displayed in the week that elapsed between the capitulation of the city and their discharge.... The

William 'Bigfoot' Wallace: depicted here in his golden years, the rugged old warrior is still festooned with an assortment of weaponry. This image suggests how he acquired his nickname. (Daughters of the Republic of Texas Library at the Alamo)

commanding general took occasion to thank them for the efficient service they had rendered, and we saw them turn their faces toward the blood-bought state they represented, with many good wishes and the hope that all honest Mexicans were a safe distance from their path.'

Taylor, however, had other problems. As 1847 began, US President James K. Polk authorized Gen. Winfield Scott's plan to end the war quickly by a strategic turning movement from the coastal port of Veracruz to Mexico City. The gambit called for most of Taylor's veterans to muster in the Tampico area, where they would board ship for Scott's amphibious expedition. The scheme left Taylor with only 5,000

Palmetto hat: rangers often found straw hats better suited to Texas summers than those made of beaver or felt. This example dates from the late 1850s. (Texas Confederate Museum, Waco)

troops of whom only a minuscule portion were regulars.

This shift of front offered Mexican Gen. Santa Anna a splendid opportunity. Learning of Scott's plans, he vowed to overwhelm Taylor's contingent before Scott could land. In a relentless forced march Santa Anna drove 20,000 men across the desert from San Luis Potosí to Encarnación, only 35 miles south of Taylor's isolated force. The gruelling midwinter march through the barren wasteland cost Santa Anna some 4,000 effectives, but with 16,000 remaining he felt confident that he could obliterate Taylor's meagre 5,000.

Taylor once again called on the rangers. Although most had departed after the fall of Monterrey, Maj. Ben McCulloch had led a company back after a recruiting trip in Texas. Relations between the general and the rangers were still strained, but with most of his force siphoned off to join Scott's army Taylor had to accept any veterans he could muster, even 'licentious' Texans. Taylor knew rangers could obtain information when others failed.

On 16 February McCulloch and 16 men routed a Mexican cavalry in the Encarnación vicinity and returned to tell Taylor that the enemy was within striking distance. This was important intelligence; but Taylor now needed to learn the enemy's strength and exact position. Again he summoned McCulloch. Riding back to Encarnación in the dark, McCulloch and seven rangers silently crept past Mexican pickets. Judging from the dimensions of the camp, McCulloch calculated the size of the enemy army; he then sent Lt. Fielding Alston and five men back to Taylor with this information while he and one ranger remained to await the dawn. As the daylight illuminated Santa Anna's encampment McCulloch made a careful count of regimental standards. Increased visibility, of course, also heightened the rangers' vulnerability. McCulloch decided to run a bluff. As nonchalantly as possible, the rangers rode past the Mexican pickets. Since the Texans were astride Mexican saddles and wore sombreros and serapes the pickets probably surmised they were *rancheros* routinely rounding up wayward cavalry mounts. Once beyond musket range the rangers galloped to report the enemy's strength and location.

Armed with McCulloch's information, Taylor withdrew to a defensive position in the narrow mountain gap some eight miles south of Saltillo, where on 22–23 February 1847 he fought the battle of Buena Vista. Both sides were staggered by their losses. Finally, however, Santa Anna, unable to break the US line, retreated with the devastated remnants of his army. Unable to surprise Taylor, he had forfeited his best chance to overwhelm the *norteamericanos*. His failure to do so was largely the result of the daring of Ben McCulloch and seven Texas Rangers.

Counter-guerrillas
Veracruz fell to the US landing force on 27 March 1847, and Winfield Scott marched westward with 8,500 men. Wherever Santa Anna attempted to block the American advance, Scott outgeneralled him and pushed forward in his relentless drive on Mexico City. With every step westward, however, Scott stretched his lines of communication to his strategic base in Veracruz. Soon Mexican partisans, the dreaded *guerrilleros*, began to threaten Scott's ability to obtain supplies and information. US regulars fell prey to the *guerrillero* mystique, which was calculated by the partisans to inflict maximum psychological damage on the invaders. Americans found the bodies of stragglers with their hearts and tongues cut out and placed on tree limbs over the corpses. Guerrillas, armed with rifles, pistols, carbines, daggers, lances, and lassoes, were far better equipped than Scott's regulars. Small wonder that Pennsylvania Volunteer Jacob Oswandel recorded that he 'would sooner face ten of the regular Mexican army than one of these outlawed guerrillas'.

Scott had to avoid a general insurrection of the Mexican populace. To that end, he attempted to calm the non-combatants with patience and courtesy while dealing harshly with the guerrillas themselves. When his regulars proved incapable of dealing with the partisans, he called on Col. Hays and his Texas Rangers to be his agents of severity.

The effect on American morale was immediate; with the Texas Rangers they now had an élite unit with a mystique to match that of the *guerrilleros*. Where the guerrillas were resplendent, the rangers were outrageous. 'They certainly were an odd-looking set of fellows, and it seems to be their aim to dress as outlandishly as possible', one regular officer remarked. 'Bobtailed coats and "long-tailed Blues", low and high crowned hats, some slouched and others Panama, with a sprinkling of black leather caps, constituting their uniforms, and a thorough coating of dust over all, and covering their huge beards gave them a savage appearance.'

'Plains Indian with shield', watercolour by German artist Friedrich Richard Petri, undated. (Texas Memorial Museum, Austin, courtesy of Mr. William Hill)

The same officer was even more impressed with ranger weaponry. 'Each man', he wrote, 'carried a rifle [and] a pair of . . . Colt's revolvers; a hundred of them could discharge a thousand shots in two minutes, and with a precision the Mexican alone could tell.' These were the new six-shot Whitneyville Walker Colts, so-called because Samuel H. Walker had worked with Sam Colt to improve the Patterson design. The 'Walker' provided a lethal edge for the Texans, for when packing a brace of these revolvers they could unleash 12 shots to the one discharged by the Mexican *escopetas*. Ranger Adjutant John Salmon Ford boasted that armed with the Walker Colt,

Placido, Chief of the Tonkawas, a veteran of Plum Creek and 'Rip' Ford's 1859 Red River campaign. (Prints and Photographs Collection, Barker Texas History Center, University of Texas at Austin)

rangers 'could beat any number the enemy could bring to bear'.

US regulars who had earlier been appalled by their methods now applauded ranger viciousness. Everywhere they rode, Texans were perceived as men of demonic malice, yet they did yeoman service as counter-insurgents. By curtailing the partisans they maintained American lines of communication and boosted American morale. Critics argued that the rangers should have demonstrated more moderation; but from the extravagance of their attire to the boldness of their leadership and the size of their Bowie knives, it was immoderation that distinguished the Texas Rangers. These were the type of men Scott required to clear his path of guerrillas; 'moderate' men could not have done the job.

EARLY STATEHOOD, 1849–1865

Juan Nepomuceno Cortina, the inveterate Río Grande raider of the late *1850s–1870s (Texas State Library, Archives Division, Austin)*

The Treaty of Guadalupe Hidalgo signed on 2 February 1848 officially ended the Mexican–American War, and rangers began to make their way home toward Texas. Now in full partnership with the United States, most Texans were proud of their new status—finally acknowledged when Mexico formally recognized the Río Grande as the national border. The cost of that acknowledgement had been high. Many rangers had paid it with their lives, including the gallant Samuel H. Walker who had fallen leading a charge of US Mounted Rifles.

The federal government and the US Army assumed responsibility for protection against the Indians and, in theory anyway, supplanted the Texas Rangers. Most returned to civilian pursuits; but the more adventurous, like Jack Hays and Ben McCulloch, joined other 'forty-niners' in the gold fields of California. The United States had established procedures for Indian control, which involved settling Indians on reservations and establishing US regulars in a line of frontier outposts. It soon became apparent, however, that federal forces were unequal to the task. Pitifully thin on the ground, garrison troops were commonly eastern recruits with no comprehension of Indian warfare. This became obvious when army commanders dispatched infantrymen to quell the Comanches, perhaps the finest light horsemen the world has ever known. Even US Dragoons were outclassed. Ranger 'Buck' Barry observed their inadequacies with obvious disgust:

'Neither the dragoons on their big and awkward chargers nor the infantry understood how to fight the Comanches. This fact the Indians soon learned and they became so active that the people began to call for someone who could cope with them. The regulars generally did not know the country and the redskins would lead them over 'hill and dale' until the troopers and their mounts were exhausted.'

Bowing to pressure from outraged Texans, the regulars requested assistance. In 1849 Gen. George M. Brooke asked Governor George T. Wood to raise three companies of rangers for a six-month stint along the frontier. These were so effective that by

1852 he had signed up a total of six companies. Among the leaders of these various contingents were several old stalwarts: R. E. Sutton, J. B. McGown, Henry McCulloch (Ben's brother), 'Bigfoot' Wallace and John Salmon Ford.

With John Coffee Hays far away in California, Ford was next in the line of succession as chief ranger. While serving as Hays's adjutant during the Mexican–American War he had written letters to the bereaved families of fallen rangers. Ford thoughtfully ended each missive with the sentiment 'Rest in Peace', but as the number of letters mounted he shortened it to 'R.I.P.', and the rangers wryly nicknamed him 'Old Rip'.

In response to continued Mexican bandit raids Texans remained vigilant along the Río Grande, a posture which created strife between the state and federal governments. In 1852 Governor Peter Hansborough Bell despatched James S. Gillett to southern Texas to organize three ranger companies. Although no funds were immediately available to pay them, Bell assured Gillett that volunteers would be mustered into federal service; failing that, the State Legislature would underwrite the units. Gillett organized the companies, but the United States Secretary of War refused to authorize their attachment to the army; Washington officials were not convinced that border forays were as serious as Texans suggested. In 1854 a few ranger companies were attached to the army but, after Washington's rebuff, the Texas Rangers began to function mainly as a state force.

Responding to Apache raids on south-western Texas in 1855, Governor Elisha M. Pease mustered three companies of Texas Rangers under frontier veteran James H. Callahan. Although members of the 'Callahan Expedition' were required to provide their own supplies and await payment from the state there was no lack of volunteers.

Indians had learned to evade the pursuit of US regulars by slipping across the border into Mexico. Callahan refused to be hampered by such fine points of international law, and brazenly led his men across the Río Grande on the heels of a fleeing war party.

In this Remington illustration, 'Rip' Ford leads a charge toward a Comanche camp on the Canadian River. (Harper's Magazine, 1896)

Not surprisingly, Mexican authorities objected to the violation of their sovereignty by units of armed Texans. The rangers, however, declined to budge until the Mexicans handed over the renegades. When their demands were rejected, rangers took on units of the Mexican army. During the fighting indignant Texans occupied the town of Piedras Negras, burned numerous buildings, and finally, in the face of overwhelming numbers, retreated across the border.

Washington officials were not pleased; neither were their counterparts in Mexico City. Governor Pease suffered a welter of criticism over this international incident, but stood by his rangers. Callahan, however, was symbolically dismissed for his impulsive invasion, though in Texas he was hailed as a hero. After he was killed in a 'personal difficulty' in 1856 grateful citizens named a county in his honour. Rangers continued to mount hot pursuits into Mexico whenever they deemed it expedient; sometimes the grounds were admittedly flimsy, and on occasion they even entered Mexico in search of runaway slaves. After the 'Callahan Expedition' a willingness

to ignore the Mexican border became something of a ranger legacy.

In 1858 Governor Hardin R. Runnels vowed to protect frontier settlers against Indian raids. By then the line of settlement had progressed well into West Texas, encroaching on Comanche hunting grounds, and the desperate tribesmen were striking back. Runnels appointed the steady 'Rip' Ford as senior ranger captain with orders to take the war to the heart of the *Comanchería*; and during the spring of 1858, there he took it.

Ford led a force of 213 men northward across the Red River as far as the Canadian River in Indian Territory. Riding with Ford's contingent were Chief Placido and several of his Tonkawa braves; these 'reserve Indians' frequently joined rangers on expeditions against the Comanches, their ancient enemies. On 12 May Ford approached a Comanche village on the south bank of the Canadian River. Warriors rode out to challenge the Texans led by Iron Jacket, a powerful medicine man whom his braves believed possessed the power to blow speeding bullets aside with his breath. His name derived from his habit of donning a rusty coat of Spanish mail.

Ford's unit charged the warriors with 'vigor and effect'. Iron Jacket fell dead, the links of his antique armour rent by ranger lead. As the Comanches retreated, Texans and Tonkawas pursued until their horses foundered. The triumph was devastating. Ford located the bodies of 76 Comanches; many more had been wounded, but Ford found it 'impossible to ascertain the number'. Of Ford's force, two were killed and three wounded. In his report to Governor Runnels, Ford lauded the conduct of his men: 'They behaved, while under fire, in a gallant and soldier-like manner, and I think that they have fully vindicated their right to be recognized as Texas Rangers of the old stamp.'

No sooner had Ford pacified the northern frontier than trouble once more erupted along the southern border. In 1859 Juan Nepomuceno Cortina led a Hispanic revolt in the lower Río Grande Valley. To his people he was a liberator; to the rangers he was just another border bandit. For a brief period Cortina

The 1861 Harper's Weekly *illustrator was clearly influenced by sensational newspaper stories. This* oft-reproduced sketch is a paradigm of mythical Texas Ranger images. *(Harper's Weekly, 1861)*

During the 1870s, long after his days of active service, retired ranger Robert Hall concocted this outlandish buckskin jacket. Many old-timers participated in the creation of the mythic stereotype by donning such fanciful 'frontier' garb for ceremonial occasions. (Dallas Historical Society)

Robert Hall's buckskin pants. Apparently invented at the same time as his jacket, this colourful article is hardly typical. Any ranger so adorned would have been laughed out of camp. (Dallas Historical Society)

occupied the town of Brownsville, only withdrawing after sacking the town and killing several Anglo citizens. Before departing Cortina vowed that he sought the restoration of all the land between the Nueces River and the Río Grande, and further proclaimed that 'our personal enemies shall not possess our lands until they have fattened it with their own gore'. After Cortina defeated W. G. Tobin's ranger company his reputation soared.

Peace was not restored to the valley until the regular army and 'Rip' Ford's company arrived. A combined force of regulars and rangers defeated Cortina at Río Grande City and drove his band across the border. Ford led several futile forays across the international boundary, but failed to apprehend the red-bearded revolutionary; he finally withdrew under orders from the new federal commander in the region, a dignified Virginian named Robert E. Lee. The rangers never captured Cortina, who continued to organize raids into Texas until the 1870s.

The war years

When the War Between the States began in 1861 most rangers left the service to fight Yankees. Ben McCulloch served as a Confederate general, and fell while leading an assault at Elkhorn Tavern. Terry's Rangers, and several other units of Texas cavalry, adopted the title, but they were not Texas Rangers in the accepted sense; the choice of that term, however, proclaimed the power of the name.

With most able-bodied men fighting out of state, the Comanches renewed their raids. In 1861 state authorities created the Frontier Battalion to provide defence against Indians but, consisting mainly of old men and young boys, the force was largely ineffective. By 1865 Plains Indians had pushed the line of settlement back a hundred miles. After Appomattox grey-clad Texans returned home to find the western counties ravaged by their old Comanche adversaries. As always, Texans called on their rangers.

Major John B. Jones, who led the Frontier Battalion in the lawless 1870s. (Prints and Photographs

Collection, Barker Texas History Center, University of Texas at Austin)

THE FRONTIER BATTALION, 1866–1890

Following the War Between the States, Texans witnessed an unprecedented escalation of violence. Vanquished veterans returned home to a shattered economy and a Reconstruction government indifferent to their plight. The only skills many of these men had were those learned in war, and some turned to their guns to make a living.

Rangers were now required not so much to combat Indians as to suppress domestic disorder. For nine years following the war, however, the organization was dormant: state officials, consisting primarily of 'carpetbagger' appointees, did not savour the notion of contingents of ex-rebels patrolling the countryside. Indian defence was relegated to federal troops and under the dynamic leadership of Ranald S. Mackenzie of the 4th Cavalry they accomplished far more than their pre-war predecessors. The fact that Col. Mackenzie employed the time-honoured ranger tactic of striking Indians deep inside their own territory was not lost on resentful Texans.

In 1873 Democrats regained control of state government, effectively ending Reconstruction in Texas. Prior to the war Texans had urged the federal government to accept the responsibility of frontier defence, but now they bitterly rejected the blue-coated troopers, especially black 'buffalo soldiers'. In their zeal to eliminate everything that smacked of Republican rule, Democrats unfairly focused their fury on some of the bravest soldiers who ever served in Texas. They made it clear, however, that they intended to restore their own institutions, one of the most treasured of which was the Texas Rangers. In his inaugural address Governor Richard Coke emphasized frontier defence and the Democratic legislature quickly passed a bill authorizing six ranging companies of 75 men each. Known as the Frontier Battalion, the unit would be led by a major who was to report directly to the adjutant general and the governor.

On 2 May 1874 Coke appointed John B. Jones as major of the Frontier Battalion. Like Hays, Jones was soft-spoken and slight of stature, but his service in the war as a member of Terry's Rangers certified him a first class fighting man. Temperate and courtly—he never touched tobacco or strong drink—Jones was a favourite of Texan ladies, one of whom was almost as enamoured of him as she was of the use of adjectives: 'I can see him now, the perfection of neatness; dark well-kept suit, white shirt, black bow tie, heavy black mustache and hair, smooth olive skin, piercing, twinkling, sparkling, penetrating black or dark eyes that seemed to see through your very soul, and seeing sympathized as he understood.'

Jones, however, was no parlour paladin. 'Major Jones was a man of great administrative and executive ability', Capt. Dan W. Roberts attested, 'and none of

the Rangers could beat him to a real live scrap with the enemy.' Less than a month after receiving his commission Jones had five companies patrolling the western frontier; by 10 July all six were in the saddle. He grasped the larger picture, and organized defence along a 400-mile perimeter. Under Jones the rangers, acting in co-ordination with the federal troopers, finally crushed the Comanches. The struggle had been costly: in each year between 1836 and 1860 Indians killed some 200 men, women, and children on the Texas frontier; between 1860 and 1875 at least 100 a year were killed or kidnapped. The advance through the expanse of Central Texas had exacted 17 white lives per mile.

The Frontier Battalion had been in service for only

Although much has been written about the bond between a ranger and his horse, a sturdy pack mule was also a vital part of the team, as revealed in this Remington illustration. (Harper's Magazine, 1896)

about five months when its numbers were reduced. Governor Coke learned that the $75,000 allocated by the legislature would not maintain the six companies for two years, the period remaining before another session met to approve additional appropriations. Bowing to economic and administrative demands, Coke reduced the number of men in each company from 75 to 40. Others might have protested such drastic cuts, but Jones and his rangers stoically bid their comrades farewell and continued to serve.

Transition into lawmen

The role of the Texas Rangers was shifting dramatically. They had traditionally been Indian fighters, but by 1875 there were few braves left to fight. Even so, Jones's rangers would not remain idle. Texas was plagued by lawlessness. The range cattle industry was beginning to pump new life into the state's war-shattered economy, but rustlers were threatening its growth. Smouldering animosities between Democratic and Republican factions divided communities and often blazed into bloody feuds. Embroiled in partisan politics themselves, local officials were powerless to keep the peace. As impartial outsiders reporting directly to the governor, rangers were ideally suited to settle regional disputes. Some rangers were uncomfortable in their new role. 'We hardly knew whether we were Rangers, or court officers', one old-timer complained. But cold percentages reflected the changing times: in 1874 the property retrieved from outlaws was worth twice that recovered from the Indians.

In February 1875 dissension generated by cattle-stealing and shady dealings erupted into the so-called Mason County War; because of the name given to masked nightriders, the conflict was also known as the 'Hoodoo War'. Governor Coke dispatched Jones and 20 men of Company A to quell the violence. When the rangers arrived on 28 September they were challenged by Sheriff John Clark and 15 of his partisan cronies. When Clark noted the ranger's cool resolve, however, he backed down. Rangers began an impartial enforcement of the law and quickly halted the killings. The presence of the rangers allowed passions to cool and prompted many of the hired gunmen to relocate to healthier climes. By 1876 the feuding had died out and rangers could report that 'Mason County is now prosperous and happy'.

The rangers also became embroiled in the Horrell–Higgins feud in Lampasas County. Having run foul of the federal authorities during Reconstruction, the Horrell brothers had fled to New Mexico, where they were involved in the 'Horrell War' in which some 17 men were killed. With their welcome worn out in New Mexico, the Horrells moved back home to Lampasas County where they settled on a ranch near John Pinckney Calhoun Higgins. 'Pink' Higgins was not a man to be trifled with either. He

In this Remington illustration a single Texas Ranger apprehends three chaparral bandits in the Nueces Strip. (Harper's Magazine, *1896*)

had once come upon a rustler who had just slaughtered one of his beeves; 'Old Pink' shot the thief, slit the animal open, and stuffed the dead man inside the carcass. Riding into town, he wryly informed citizens that if they would visit his range they could witness the peculiar spectacle of a cow giving birth to a man. Local cattle thieves apparently did not share Pink's sense of humour, and when the story made the rounds most left the county.

That trouble should arise between these tumultuous clans was as natural as a tussle among tomcats. Pink believed the Horrells were stealing his stock, and on 22 January 1877 he shot and killed Merritt Horrell in a local saloon. The Horrells swore vengeance, but the Higginses struck first when they waylaid Tom and Mart Horrell that March; Tom was seriously wounded, but Mart coolly stood off his concealed attackers and finally forced them to retreat. On 14 June both factions happened to be in the town of Lampasas at the same time, and bystanders ducked for cover as gunplay unsettled the business district.

A personal affray was considered a man's own business, but when it threatened the safety of women and children on a public street it was time to call in the rangers. On 12 July Maj. Jones arrived in Lampasas with 15 men. He arrested the leading members of both families, and reported: 'Have no doubt that I will hold them and protect them until they are disposed of according to law, and believe that both parties will submit quietly to the decision.' Jones proved a peacemaker as well as a warrior. With patience, reason, and tact he served as mediator for both sides. His diplomacy culminated in a document in which the two families agreed to 'eradicate all enmity'.

Despite its record of achievement, the Frontier Battalion did not win every encounter. Events leading to the El Paso Salt War began in 1872 when Missouri lawyer Charles H. Howard acquired title to salt deposits 100 miles east of El Paso. For generations local Hispanics had regarded the salt as a public resource, and they bitterly resented its appropriation for private profit. In 1874 Howard became a

district judge and misused his position against political rival Louis Cardis, who represented Hispanic interests and controlled the Mexican electorate. Threats were made against Howard and several of his business associates. On 10 October 1877 Howard responded by killing Cardis in an El Paso emporium. Mexicans demanded justice, but Anglo peace officers were unwilling to arrest a district judge.

Maj. Jones had no such qualms. Soon after arriving in El Paso he had Judge Howard arraigned for the murder of Cardis. He then set about organizing local volunteers into a detachment of rangers. He placed Lt. John B. Tays in command at San Elizario, the hub of the tumult. With peace temporarily restored and the newly-raised company of rangers on duty, Jones left town. He should have stayed.

On or about 1 December 1877 outraged Mexicans from across the border raided the area, killing two of Howard's cronies. The judge, who was out on bail, and several of his associates took refuge inside ranger

In 1876 Ranger A. M. Gildea posed in an Eagle Pass studio. He obviously favoured Hispanic fashions: note the elaborately embroidered jacket and the brightly coloured ribbon outlining the brim of his hat. (Daughters of the Republic of Texas Library at the Alamo, San Antonio)

headquarters at San Elizario. The mob demanded that Tays turn over Howard. When he refused the Mexicans laid siege to the building. On the fifth day of the siege Howard gave himself up in order to save the members of his party. Believing that the judge was to be granted safe conduct, Tays also surrendered—the first and only time a ranger company ever capitulated. Despite pledges of good faith, on 17 December Howard and two of his agents were placed against the nearest wall and shot by a Mexican firing squad. The Mexicans harboured no ill will toward Tays and his rangers, who were allowed to depart without weapons. Afterwards, the mob looted San Elizario. The Texas Rangers were embarrassed by this episode, but learned three hard lessons: never give up your weapons, never surrender a prisoner to a mob, and—whatever the odds—keep fighting.

Sam Bass

Rangers also trailed a number of renowned outlaws. One of these was the personable Sam Bass, who came to Texas from Indiana in 1870. Bass began 'sporting on horses' and was soon in need of money. In 1876 he rode up the trail to Montana on a cattle drive, ending up in the rugged mining town of Deadwood where he soon squandered his wages at the card tables. The next year the desperate youth held up seven stagecoaches. Bass soon advanced to robbing trains, which became his speciality. He returned to Texas and established himself as leader of an outlaw band, which robbed two stagecoaches and four trains during the spring of 1878.

The Texas Rangers swore to bring Bass in. They came close to capturing the desperado on several occasions, but the wily Bass managed to keep one step ahead. At last the rangers were able to capture one of the Bass gang, but freed him on the condition that he rejoin the band as their agent. In July 1878 rangers received word from their inside man that Bass intended to rob a bank in the town of Round Rock, some 20 miles north of Austin. Maj. Jones and the rangers were waiting. In the shoot-out that followed on 19 July 1878 they gunned down one of the outlaws. Bass himself took several bullets, but managed a getaway. He did not get far. After he was discovered and taken into custody the mortally wounded outlaw came clean. 'Yes, I am Sam Bass', he told a reporter. 'I'm shot to pieces, and there's no use to deny it.'

Sam Bass as he appeared at the age of 16—the only documented picture of the famous outlaw known to exist. (Prints and Photographs Collection, Barker Texas History Center, University of Texas at Austin)

Nevertheless, he steadfastly refused to reveal any information concerning his accomplices, explaining 'it's agin my profession to blow on my pals. If a man knows anything, he ought to die with it in him'. On 21 July, true to his code, the tight-lipped bandit did just that.

Sam Bass was only one of many criminals whose careers were abruptly ended by Maj. Jones and the Frontier Battalion. These rangers established law in a part of the state where it was previously unknown. While the Frontier Battalion patrolled western counties, however, another equally famous ranger unit was engaged in the nefarious 'Nueces Strip' of South Texas.

McNELLY'S RANGERS, 1874–1890

In 1874 the Texas Legislature created two bodies of Texas Rangers: the Frontier Battalion under Maj. Jones, and the Special Force under Capt. Leander H. McNelly. Politicians in Austin understood that lawlessness along the Mexican border took a different form from that in West Texas, and constituted the Special Force to deal with special problems.

McNelly was a curious mixture of propriety and severity. Like many great ranger captains, he did not look the role. George Durham, who served under him, maintained that McNelly 'dressed neat as a pin' and simply from appearances he 'could have been a preacher. A puny one at that'. The captain's demeanour, however, masked an indomitable resolve. During the war he led a band of Confederate partisans and saw much hard fighting in Louisiana. During his wartime travails McNelly contracted tuberculosis and thereafter had to take long furloughs to recover his health. He returned to Texas near the end of the conflict, and his was among the last Confederate units to surrender.

Despite his war record he was offered, and accepted, a position in the State Police, an arm of the Radical Republican government. Most Texans loathed the organization and it was repudiated the instant Democrats regained control in 1873. That Texans were willing to overlook McNelly's participation in the State Police was a testament to the man's ability and personal integrity.

In 1874 NcNelly and his rangers were instrumental in quelling the violence associated with the Sutton–Taylor Feud in Dewitt County. Afterwards he moved southward into the region between the Río Grande and the Nueces River, the area known as the Nueces Strip. On 26 March 1875 a well-organized band of border raiders struck the South Texas hamlet of Nuecestown, where they made off with 18 Dick Heye saddles—which Durham called the 'Cadillacs of the saddle world'. McNelly instructed local shop keepers to sell no more Dick Heye saddles, and then issued orders to First Sergeant John B. Armstrong:

Captain Leander H. McNelly, the ruthless tamer of the Nueces Strip, whose three years in command of the Special Force in the mid-1870s left an indelible impression. (Prints and Photographs Collection, Barker Texas History Center, University of Texas at Austin)

'Describe those saddles to the rangers. Make sure they understand exactly. Then order them to empty those saddles on sight. No palavering with the riders. Empty them. Leave the men where you drop them, and bring the saddles to camp.'

Such direct action was typical of McNelly's tactics. Still, events called for extreme measures. Juan Cortina's bands were still terrorizing Anglo Texans, who in turn organized vigilante groups that victimized local *tejanos*, for the most part peaceful herders. Violence in the Nueces Strip was escalating; the number of bandits, both Mexican and Texan, began to surpass honest folk. McNelly lost no time; he dispersed bodies of armed civilians, and took the fight to Cortina's men when they could be ferreted out.

His methods were brutal, but his standards for rangers were rigorous. Once when he was offered an array of the newest repeating rifles, he declined them in favour of the old-fashioned .50 calibre Sharps buffalo gun. 'Sharps, Captain?' the dumbfounded merchant inquired. 'I thought you were going man hunting—not buffalo. Those heavy, single-shot Sharps—whew! When you hit a buffalo, he's yours. If you miss, you can reload. If you miss a man ...' The captain had heard enough: he snapped, 'I don't want men who miss.'

If NcNelly was hard on his rangers, he was even harder on outlaws. He reinstituted the old Spanish practice of *la ley de fuga*, which prescribed that a prisoner was to be summarily shot in the event of a rescue attempt. In the absence of courts and judges

McNelly practised the Old Testament law of 'an eye for an eye'. As one of his rangers explained it: 'Those Nueces outlaws didn't fight by any books. Neither did Captain McNelly. They made their own rules, and the Captain made his. They didn't mind killing. Neither did Captain McNelly. They didn't take prisoners. Neither did Captain McNelly.'

In 1875 the captain's zeal almost provoked an international incident during the so-called Las Cuevas War. He led his rangers across the Río Grande in hot pursuit of cattle thieves, and attacked a ranch near the border town of Las Cuevas which he thought was the rustlers' hideout. As it turned out, it

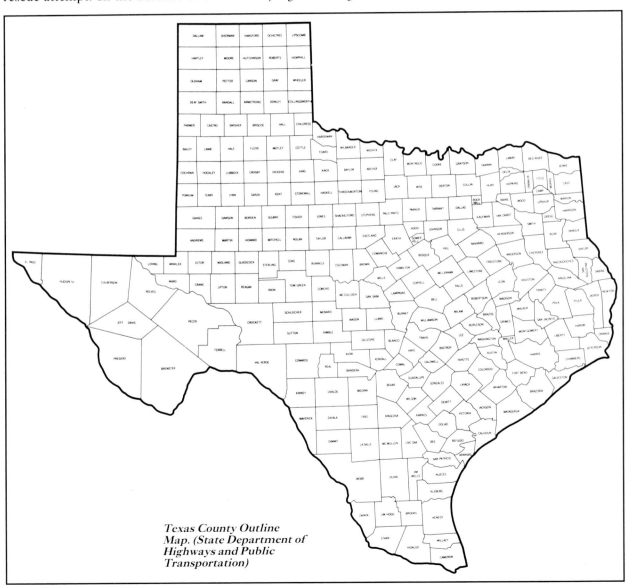

Texas County Outline Map. (State Department of Highways and Public Transportation)

was the wrong ranch, and several honest *vaqueros* were gunned down; understandably, local Mexicans were outraged. Several hundred soldiers and villagers assailed the rangers, but NcNelly's 30 men dug in on the south bank of the Río Grande and held them off.

Across the border was an anxious contingent of US regulars. They had explicit orders from the State Department not to enter Mexico, and tried to coax the angry Texans back across the river before a full-scale war ensued. A messenger swam the narrow river with a telegram to McNelly from the United States Secretary of War, exhorting the rangers to return to Texas and affirming that if they were attacked on Mexican soil the regulars would not support them. McNelly's reply was succinct: 'I shall remain in Mexico with my Rangers . . . and will cross back at my own discretion. Give my compliments to the secretary of war and tell him and the United States soldiers to go to hell.'

In the face of overwhelming numbers, McNelly brazenly told the Mexicans that if they did not agree to return the pilfered cattle within the hour he would unleash his rangers on the town. Amazingly, the Mexicans yielded to McNelly's demands and subsequently the rangers returned to Texas driving 75 head of stolen stock.

On 26 January 1877 McNelly's iron will finally succumbed to tuberculosis. He had been a Texas Ranger less than three years, but in that time he secured a place in the pantheon of ranger leaders second only to Jack Hays. A legion of detractors decried his ruthless methods, but none could question his accomplishments: NcNelly got the job done. Among his generation of Texans that was the only standard that mattered.

During the summer of 1876, when McNelly became too ill to fork a saddle, Lt. Lee Hall took

In 1888 this young bride posed with her husband and the rest of Sam Murry's Company B. Note that she too bears a Winchester repeating rifle. (Prints and Photographs Collection, Barker Texas History Center, University of Texas at Austin)

Ranger Sergeant W. J. L. Sullivan. Note the decorative needlework on the cuffs of his gauntlets. Like most rangers, Sullivan reserved the cartridge loops in his gun belt for rifle ammunition. (Twelve Years in the Saddle, Archives Division, Texas State Library, Austin)

command of the Special Force. By that time the emphasis of the company's endeavours had shifted from fighting Mexican bandits to quashing Anglo renegades. Old feuds reignited, and a spirit of suspicion and disorder prevailed throughout South Texas. These were also the days of the great cattle drives, creating abundant opportunity for roving cattle rustlers. Quietly but firmly, Hall set about restoring order. His personal style was not as imperious nor as controversial as McNelly's, a difference welcomed by state officials.

Adjutant General William Steele compiled a lengthy album giving the names and descriptions of fugitive outlaws. Armed with the 'Crime Book', Hall and the other ranger captains were thereafter able to devote their energies to apprehending known criminals rather than rousting out doubtful suspects. The men who had served under McNelly—who began calling themselves 'Little McNellys'— never believed that Hall completely filled the old captain's boots. Nevertheless, one Goliad County citizen expressed his fervent appreciation of Hall in a letter to the governor:

'Through the inefficiency of our sheriff our town and county had become a rendezvous of escaped convicts, cutthroats, outlaws, and murderers riding through our streets at night, shooting through business houses and private dwellings, imperiling the lives of our women and children. . . . Lieutenant Hall had come an entire stranger, had taken in the situation at a glance and applied the remedy which caused the bold bad men to flee to parts unknown.' The events in Goliad County were common to numerous South Texas localities.

John Wesley Hardin

One McNelly-trained ranger gained fame as the captor of John Wesley Hardin, thought by many to be the 'most notorious desperado Texas ever produced'. A stout man with a massive moustache, John B. Armstrong had served as first sergeant of the Special Force and was the survivor of several Nueces Strip shoot-outs, including the Las Cuevas stand-off. McNelly was his model and, like his mentor, Armstrong did not hesitate to employ severe methods if necessity demanded.

Texas Rangers accepted that extreme sanctions would almost certainly be required to bring in Hardin, widely known as a wilful killer. Although he had been too young to fight in the war, Hardin cast

John Wesley Hardin, perhaps the worst of all Texan badmen, finally captured by Ranger John B. Armstrong. (Prints and Photographs Collection, Barker Texas History Center, University of Texas at Austin)

Charles August Johnson of Company E, Frontier Battalion, poses with his favourite mount in 1892. (Archives Division, Texas State Library, Austin)

Williamson's Rangers, 1836
1: Major Robert McAlpin Williamson
2: Ranger Private
3: Ranger Private

2   1   3   A

The Battle of Plum Creek, 1840
1: Comanche Warrior
2: Texas Ranger

Los Diablos Tejanos, 1847
1: Captain Ben McCulloch
2: Ranger Sergeant
3: Ranger Lieutenant
4: Mexican Peon

C

Hays's Rangers, 1848
1: Colonel John C. 'Jack' Hays
2: Mexican Guerrillero
3: Texas Ranger Private
4: Tortillera

D

2

3

Canadian River Campaign, 1858
1: Captain John S. 'Rip' Ford
2: Iron Jacket
3: Ranger Private

E

1

2

3

Frontier Defence, 1864
1: Ranger Captain
2: Ranger Private
3: Ranger Sergeant

F

Frontier Battalion, c.1880
1: Major John B. Jones
2: Ranger Private
3: Ranger Private

G

McNelly's Rangers, 1876
1: Captain Leander H. McNelly
2: Ranger Sergeant
3: Ranger Private
4: Neuces Strip outlaw

H

Texas Rangers, 1915–30
1: Border Ranger, 1915
2: Captain Jerry Gray, 1921
3: Ranger C. L. 'Blackie' Blackwell, 1921

I

Texas Ranger Captains, 1930–50
1: Adjutant General William Warren Sterling, c.1930
2: Captain Francis Augustus Hamer, c.1932
3: Captain Manuel T. 'Lone Wolf' Gonzaullas, c.1950

Modern Texas Rangers, 1970-90
1: Ranger Aubrey D. Bryce
2: Ranger Ron Stewart
3: Captain Jack Dean

K

himself in the role of defender of the 'Southern cause'. The son of a Methodist preacher, he killed his first man when he was 15 years old and added six more to his score by his 17th birthday. In May 1874 Hardin gunned down Deputy Sheriff Charles Webb, and thereafter appeared on wanted posters throughout the state. With every lawman in Texas after him the killer fled to Alabama and Florida. Along the way he added six positive and two possible names to his list of victims.

Despite Hardin's standing as a lethal gunman, Armstrong requested the case and then tracked his man throughout the south. On 23 July 1877 he cornered his quarry on a train in Pensacola, Florida. Armstrong boarded a rail car to face the man he had travelled hundreds of miles to apprehend. Hardin was not alone: four compatriots sat nearby, but Armstrong would not be deterred by such odds. Drawing his long-barrelled Colt .45, Armstrong approached the seated fugitive. Hardin immediately guessed this lawman's employer: 'Texas, by God!' he shouted. One of Hardin's companions fired a bullet through Armstrong's hat; Armstrong blew a hole through his chest. Hardin drew his pistol, but it became caught on his suspenders and the loss of that split second sealed his fate: as he struggled to extricate his revolver, Armstrong knocked him cold with the seven-inch barrel of his Colt. Hardin crumpled to the floor and the ranger covered the

Company E, Texas Rangers Frontier Battalion, 1892. (Texas

State Library, Archives Division, Austin)

three remaining men, who quickly dropped their pistols. When Hardin regained consciousness he was in custody on his way back to Texas. Armstrong despatched a terse telegram to Austin: 'Arrested John Wesley Hardin, Pensacola, Florida, this p.m. He had four men with him. Had some lively shooting. One of their number killed, all the rest captured.' Armstrong also sent the state's criminal element a portentous message: kill a Texas lawman and there was no place where rangers would not stalk you.

Hardin was sentenced to 25 years in prison for killing Deputy Sheriff Webb. During his term he studied law, supervised the prison Sunday school, and made several escape attempts. When pardoned in 1894 Hardin was admitted to the bar, and for a time his conduct was exemplary. The next year he travelled to El Paso to serve as attorney. While there, however, he fell in with the gambling crowd, began drinking heavily, and exhibited a 'quarrelsome disposition'. On 19 August 1895 Hardin was shaking dice in an El Paso saloon when John Selman, a man he had offended, casually shot him in the back of the head. Thus ended the career of a killer who boasted between 25 and 30 notches on his pistol grips. Inexplicably, Hardin became a hero to many; but Texas Rangers never numbered among his fans.

PROGRESS AND CRISIS, 1891–1934

In 1893 Frederick Jackson Turner delivered his seminal address, 'The Significance of the Frontier in American History'. Turner's 'frontier thesis' argued that with free public lands depleted and Indians settled on government reservations, the process of westward expansion that had indelibly stamped the American character had reached its natural conclusion. Texas Rangers patrolling remote reaches of West Texas would have found it difficult to accept the Wisconsin professor's conclusions, for there the old frontier habits of independence and lawlessness were still in clear evidence. Yet the more astute rangers could feel the sharp winds of change. The Frontier Battalion had been disbanded in 1891, the same year that Maj. Jones had died. In truth, the end had come not with its leader's death, but simply because the unit had outlived its usefulness.

Nevertheless, the sparsely settled regions of southwest Texas granted safe haven for American outlaws and Mexican bandits, who still pillaged both sides of the border. The few local peace officers were ill-equipped to enforce the law and maintain order without help, and Texas Rangers stood ready to provide it. In 1894–95 they rode 173,381 miles, arrested 676 suspects, rounded up and returned 2,856 head of stolen livestock, and supported local lawmen on a total of 162 occasions.

Captain Hughes and Company D, Frontier Battalion, mounted for an *expedition. (Archives Division, Texas State Library, Austin)*

In July 1901 the state legislature drafted a new law that reflected the changing role of the organization, authorizing only four companies of a maximum of 20 men each. The new ranger force still reported directly to the governor, but existed 'for the purpose of protecting the frontier against marauding or thieving parties, and for the suppression of lawlessness and crime throughout the state'. Conceived as a partisan combat unit, the Texas Rangers were now unquestionably a state police agency.

Rangers maintained certain traditions regardless. Captains still selected their own men, who still steadfastly refused to wear a uniform—not even a regular badge. They often acted independently, and their methods were often brutal. Capt. J. A. Brooks ran Company A out of Alice; Capt. W. J. McDonald was stationed in Amarillo with Company B; Capt. John H. Rogers commanded Company C at Fort Hancock; and Capt. John R. Hughes, the 'Border Boss', patrolled the area around El Paso at the head of Company D.

Capt. Bill McDonald was one of the new captains cut out of old cloth. He was a complete stranger to fear; one admirer proclaimed that 'Bill McDonald would charge hell with a bucket of water'. Also an accomplished raconteur, McDonald planted the seed that grew into the 'One Ranger-One Riot' legend. As McDonald told it, he was dispatched to Dallas to stop an illegal boxing match, and was greeted at the railroad depot by the distressed mayor. Glancing about the station, the nervous official inquired: 'Where are the others?'—to which McDonald supposedly replied, 'Hell! ain't I enough? There's only one prize-fight!' Retold over the years, various versions became so embellished that the true story

will probably never be known. He also coined the phrase that became the unofficial ranger creed: 'No man in the wrong can stand up against a fellow that's in the right and keeps on a-comin'.' Although he achieved the widest fame, McDonald's record was probably not superior to that of any other ranger captain of his time. He did, however, possess a better understanding of public relations.

During the Mexican Revolution that began in 1910 and rekindled intermittently for decades thereafter unrest frequently swept northward across the Río Grande. Mexican revolutionaries and renegades commonly raided the Big Bend region in search of arms and provisions, and rangers who patrolled that isolated sector engaged them on several occasions.

Tensions along the border reached a boiling point when Texans learned of the 'Plan of San Diego'. This was a conspiracy that called for Mexicans along both sides of the border to 'liberate' Texas, New Mexico, Arizona, and California by installing an independent republic 'which at an appropriate time would seek annexation with Mexico'. The scheme insisted on the deaths of every North American over the age of 16 except for women and old men. The mere thought that the decision of San Jacinto might be undone chilled and entraged Texans. Citizens of Mexican descent became suspect overnight.

Expansion and abuse

During World War I Governors Oscar B. Colquit and James E. 'Pa' Ferguson increased the Texas

Captain G. H. Schmitt's company at a Fort Worth railroad strike in 1886. *(Archives Division, Texas State Library, Austin)*

Company D, Frontier Battalion, along with a Mexican prisoner, sit for a photograph in 1894. Captain John R. Hughes is seated in the chair at right; the cheerless captive sits unarmed at far left. Upon seeing this photograph Hughes dismissed George Tucker, the man sitting next to the prisoner, for leaving his revolver unguarded and within reach of a desperate felon. A few days later, having taught young Tucker a critical lesson, the captain rehired him. (Archives Division, Texas State Library, Austin)

Rangers to 1,000 men, and quality, predictably, fell short of quantity. Several men entered the ranks who under normal circumstances would have been rejected out of hand; some were granted ranger status for political favours. Abuses were inevitable. In 1917, during the course of one punitive strike across the border, as many as 20 innocent Mexicans were reportedly killed. The heaviest abuse, however, fell on Mexican–American inhabitants of the Río Grande Valley, many of whom were roughed up and forced from their homes. Many *tejanos* were arrested for no apparent cause, and later shot 'while trying to escape'.

In 1918 Washington lawmakers passed National Prohibition, which presented the rangers with a new series of dilemmas. The Eighteenth Amendment may

have declared all distilled spirits illegal, but 'bootleg-gers' nonetheless began a lucrative trade in smuggled liquor. For Mexican distillers the lure of customers just across the border was irresistible; smugglers known as 'horsebackers' or *tequileros* slipped across the Río Grande nightly. Many rangers believed the law to be ludicrous, but the better ones enforced it regardless of their personal views, and clashes between rangers and armed *tequileros* were practically an everyday occurrence.

The Canales purge
Paranoia and patronage appeared to be the ruling passions among the politicians in Austin. With the original rangers so outnumbered by governor-appointed 'Special Rangers' the victimization of honest citizens continued unabated. In January 1919 State Representative J. T. Canales of Brownsville initiated a legislative inquiry into numerous ranger abuses. 'I am not an enemy to the Ranger force', he insisted. 'I merely want the personnel purified; I want efficiency, not destruction.' Canales made 18 charges against the force, the more serious of which included brutal physical assault, torture, and the summary execution of prisoners. Witnesses alleged that between 1914 and 1918 rangers had killed as many as 5,000 people, nearly all of Mexican descent.

As a result of the hearings the Texas Rangers were reduced to four companies, each consisting of 15 men, a sergeant and a captain. While the state retained a core of experienced professionals, those who had been 'arbitrary and overbearing in the discharge of their duties' were ejected from the service. Although the Canales investigation was an embarrassing ordeal for the institution, nearly all agreed that much good had ultimately resulted.

The boom years
The 'Roaring 20s' saw Texas Rangers enter the automobile age to meet new law enforcement challenges. Still active in rural regions, rangers increasingly travelled to urban centres. A labour dispute brought units to Galveston in 1920; while there the rangers performed a multitude of duties, from guarding property during strikes to delivering cita-

Company B, Frontier Battalion. Only three rangers are dressed in frontier style; the rest could easily pass for bank tellers. Note the black teamster at lower left; his appearance in the company portrait would seem evidence that the other men considered him a full participant of the unit. Clearly, his bearing bespeaks pride of membership. (Daughters of the Republic of Texas Library at the Alamo, San Antonio)

Captain Bill McDonald, who led Company B at Amarillo in the early 1900s. (Archives Division, Texas State Archives, Austin)

Texas Ranger mounted for duty, c.1889. (Prints and Photographs Collection, *Barker Texas History Center, University of Texas at Austin)*

people than the local jail could accommodate. In such cases he resorted to his 'trotline', a lengthy, heavy-duty chain to which lighter trace chains were attached. Dozens were latched to the chain, and conditions proved uncomfortable and humbling as locals jeered at the captives. Gonzaullas recalled: 'When they needed to go to a restroom there wasn't any, so they just passed the bucket.' 'Lone Wolf' was always a gentleman, however—at least by Texas standards. Trace chains were locked around the men's necks but around the ankles of the females out of courtesy to the 'ladies'. A majority of the offenders would be released from the 'trotline' if they promised to leave town by sundown, an arrangement which normally suited all concerned.

In 1932 politics once again disrupted the ranger force. Adjutant General William Warren Sterling and a majority of the rangers supported the incumbent, Governor Ross Sterling, in his bid for re-election against Miriam A. 'Ma' Ferguson. When Governor Sterling lost, Adjutant General Sterling and some 40 rangers quit rather than serve the Ferguson administration. There was no need to worry; three days after taking office the new governor spitefully fired the 44 rangers who had not already resigned. In their place she installed a motley cadre of Ferguson cronies, some of whom had criminal records. The outcome of such heedless patronage was predictable: 'Ferguson Rangers' instantly became a term of ridicule. One disgusted newspaperman reported: 'A ranger commission and a nickel will get you a cup of coffee anywhere in Texas.' Not surprisingly, lawbreakers took advantage of the absence of an effective ranger force. Felons such as George 'Machine Gun' Kelly, Raymond Hamilton, Joe Palmer, and the deadly duo of Clyde Barrow and Bonnie Parker 'shuttled between distant cities like commuters'.

Bonnie and Clyde

Officials now appreciated that only men of proven experience and ability could hope to quell the growing tide of violence. Texas Prison System Manager Lee Simmons enlisted ex-ranger Frank Hamer to hound 'mad-dog killers' Barrow and Parker 'until they were captured or put out of business'. Hamer enlisted the assistance of former ranger B. M. 'Manny' Gault, who had served under him in

tions for speeding. Across the state 'bootleggers' and their patrons flagrantly violated Prohibition laws. Gambling houses and 'gin joints' sprang up overnight, and rangers often shut them down just as quickly.

The oil boom of the 1920s and 1930s brought unprecedented wealth to the state and became a permanent part of the Texas myth. It also brought an assortment of 'bunco artists', prostitutes, gamblers, and various other ne'er-do-wells to the numerous boom towns. Texas Rangers were rushed in to enforce order.

One of the most effective and colourful was M. T. 'Lone Wolf' Gonzaullas. He obtained that nickname while stationed along the Mexican border because, as he once related, 'I went into lots of fights by myself, and I came out by myself too!' During a sweep of a busy boom town Gonzaullas often arrested more

Company A, Texas Rangers, on duty in 1905. Note the chuck wagon in the background. (Archives Division, Texas State Library, Austin)

Headquarters Company. For 102 days Hamer and Gault tracked the pair. The leads finally brought them to a country road near the sleepy hamlet of Plain Dealing, Louisiana. There, on 23 May 1934, Hamer and Gault, leading a team of local deputies, intercepted their prey. Hamer recognized the fugitives inside their stolen getaway car and shouted the command to open fire. A fusillade of machine gun and rifle fire riddled the vehicle. An inspection of the sedan's bloody interior confirmed that the pair had indeed been put out of business.

Even though Hammer and Gault had tracked and killed Bonnie and Clyde as special investigators of the Texas Prison System, the public well remembered where they had received their training. Repelled by the incompetence and graft of the 'Ferguson Rangers', Texans demanded their expulsion. During the 1934 gubernatorial race reform of the Texas Rangers proved a leading campaign issue. Candidate James V. Allred promised a complete overhauling of the ranger force. His victory initiated a period of much-needed reform and modernization.

THE MODERN TEXAS RANGERS, 1935–1991

Soon after taking office in 1935 Governor Allred revoked the commissions of the 'Ferguson Rangers' and later that year the Texas Senate proposed the creation of the Department of Public Safety (DPS). On 10 August 1935 the DPS commenced operation and the Texas Rangers were transferred from the Adjutant General's Department to the new bureau. Professor Walter Prescott Webb, historian and chronicler of the rangers, predicted the organization's collapse under DPS administration. 'As time goes on', he speculated, 'the functions of the un-uniformed Texas Rangers will gradually slip away'.

Webb was wrong. The organization was now smaller, but the quality of personnel was better than it had been in years. Moreover, under the new administrative system, the force ceased to be a

political pawn. Rangers were organized into five companies with veteran Tom Hickman as senior captain. 'Lone Wolf' Gonzaullas directed the Bureau of Intelligence, which was charged with gathering and analysing evidence at crime scenes. Rangers began to enjoy state-of-the-art techniques of criminal investigation. Gonzaullas asserted that 'scientific methods are proving to be more effective than any "third degree"', and the events of 1938 affirmed his conviction. That year evidence furnished by his crime lab dispatched 14 felons to the electric chair and led to sentences totalling 4,800 years.

When the Second World War began in 1939 Frank Hamer saw no point in waiting for his country to declare hostilities. Upon learning that Nazi agents were being parachuted into England, he offered 50 ex-rangers to provide coastal protection and thwart sabotage. On 5 September 1939 Hamer received the following telegram: 'The King greatly appreciates your offer. Please apply British Embassy, Washington'. Hamer was busy making the necessary arrangements when the US State Department, anxious to preserve its neutral status, quashed the endeavour.

Nevertheless, rangers did their part during the war. From 1942 to 1945 more than 45,000 prisoners of war were interned in Texas, and rangers occasionally tracked escapees. When the US Rangers fought their way on to the Normandy beaches German media mistakenly recounted that they were Texas Rangers. This report greatly unsettled both German soldiers and civilians, and the Reich Minister of Propaganda himself subsequently corrected the story.

Texas grew rapidly in the post-war years; the 1950 census revealed that it had become an urban state, meaning that for the first time more citizens lived in urban than rural areas. Large concentrations of people generated new law enforcement challenges, and the DPS and the Texas Rangers met them head-on. In 1949 the State Legislature had approved construction of a new DPS headquarters building in Austin. That same year the department acquired its first airplane, and a ranger became its first pilot-investigator. Statistics demonstrated the burgeoning role of the Texas Rangers: in 1935 the rangers participated in 255 cases; in 1955 they handled 16,701 cases.

Exploits during the 1950s further strengthened the Texas Ranger legend. When patients at the Rusk Hospital for the Criminally Insane took hostages and threatened to kill them, Ranger Capt. R. A. 'Bob' Crowder entered the facility alone; after a calm discussion with the leader of the mob, Crowder persuaded the other inmates to capitulate. None of the hostages nor the patients were harmed. Rangers also provided a steady presence when opponents of school integration threatened violence. Local thugs eager to harass black children proved less willing to confront Texas Rangers.

In 1967 the force and its tactics once more came under fire. In the late 1960s many Americans questioned historic values; it was the time of long hair, free love, and Acid Rock. Perhaps it was inevitable that an institution as rooted in tradition as the Texas Rangers would become a target for protest. Rangers personified the no-nonsense approach to law enforcement, and were summoned when local officers had to face dangerous felons. As one old hand observed: 'Whenever there's a mean ass, then they call on us.'

That hard-boiled outlook became part of the problem when Mexican–American migrant farm workers went on strike in the Río Grande Valley. Union members threatened to shut down public transportation and officers in Starr County requested assistance. Relying on time-honoured methods, rangers 'enforced the law by physical persuasion'. But these were not the hard cases with whom they normally dealt, being for the most part peaceful protesters working for social change. Soon charges of civil rights violations and discrimination arose from protesters, politicians, and the press. 'The Rangers may indeed now patrol in automobiles instead of on horses', one Minnesota professor chided, 'but unfor-

tunately their minds still seem to work in a rigid nineteenth-century mode. The times have passed them by, and they still believe that enforcement by fear and at pistol point is good police practice.' Although overstated, such criticism was to some degree justified; rangers were ill-trained to recognize the shadow area between the written law and social trends. One ranger later admitted as much when he remarked that the force had endeavoured 'to cope with current problems by using yesterdays' tools'. As in the 1919 Canales investigation, contention initiated reform, and since 1967 Texas Rangers have not been deployed during labour disputes.

The modern ranger is the élite of Texas law enforcement. To even be considered for the force an officer must have had at least eight years of commissioned experience, including two years with the DPS. Additionally he must have a minimum of 60 hours of college credit. Officials grant appointments based on competitive examination and individual interviews.

Unidentified Texas Ranger, 1920s. Although this cigar-chomping ranger now patrols in an automobile rather than on horseback, he still stuffs riding pants into cowboy boots. Note also the broad and fully stocked gunbelt. The notice painted on the spare tyre cover, 'I AM THE LAW TO-DAY', is a message to local law officials as well as local hoods; as agents of the state, Texas Rangers superseded town and county authorities. (Archives Division, Texas State Library, Austin)

Today's rangers possess better education, training, and hardware than their predecessors. In 1987 the average ranger was 45 years of age, and 28 had undergraduate degrees; two boasted Master's degrees. Every ranger is required to attend a minimum of 40 hours of in-service training annually, but most far exceed that requirement.

Rangers still handle the most perilous cases, and they stay ready. Every ranger is issued a service revolver, 12-gauge shotgun, and Ruger semi-automatic rifle. If more firepower is required each of the six companies is equipped with sniper rifles, infrared scopes, tear gas guns, gas masks and grenades.

Visitors to the State Cemetery in Austin often overlook one dilapidated headstone. The elements have eroded the inscription, but the determined may still make it out:

BIG FOOT
WALLACE
HERE LIES HE WHO
SPENT HIS MANHOOD
DEFENDING THE HOMES
OF TEXAS
BRAVE HONEST
AND FAITHFUL

Since 1823 Texas Rangers have defended the homes of Texas, and while they have swapped their horses for patrol cars and helicopters, the quality of their manhood remains unchanged. Texans are aware of their achievements and are appreciative; when the author paid his respects on a chilly January day in 1991, fresh flowers rested on Bigfoot's grave.

THE PLATES

A: Williamson's Rangers, 1836
A1: Major Robert McAlpin Williamson
A lawyer, Williamson normally dressed in the apparel favoured by his profession; while commanding the Texas Rangers, however, he dressed the part of a rough-hewn frontiersman. Prior to the battle of San

Captain Jerry Gray, c.1921.
(Prints and Photographs
Collection, Barker Texas

History Center, University
of Texas at Austin)

Five Ranger Captains, 1932: an Austin photographer captured this gathering of rangers whose combined service stretched from 1876 to 1933. Seated, Captain Dan W. Roberts; standing, from left to right, Captain J. A. Brooks, Adjutant General William W. Sterling, Captain Frank A. Hamer, and Captain John R. Hughes. (Archives Division, Texas State Library, Austin)

Jacinto Williamson reportedly wore a 'suit of buckskin', smudged and stiff from the elements, and a fur cap with no fewer than nine coon tails attached. After the war 'Three-Legged Willie' had his trousers tailored to cover his wooden appendage, but it is unlikely that he would have bothered to style his buckskins in such a manner. Like many rangers, Williamson is shown here with a double-barrelled shotgun, which was far easier to fire from horseback than the vaunted long rifle.

A2: Ranger Private

This simply-clothed farmer wears shirt and trousers home made of a material called linsey-woolsey, or more commonly linsey, which was originally woven of linen and wool. Cotton and wool were preferred in Texas, but the name stuck. One account told how frontier women 'carded and spun wool into rolls and yarn and used the cotton as warp and the wool as woof, and made a fine quality of homemade [linsey], which was dyed black with walnut bark and made into coats, vests and pants, which was of great benefit and highly appreciated'. The well-worn brogans are similar to those seen throughout the South during the 1830s. His canteen is fashioned from a native gourd.

This man does carry a long rifle but, unlike the more expensive models, it is of the no-frills variety.

A3: Ranger Private

Not all Texas Rangers were backwoodsmen; this figure illustrates a well-to-do planter or attorney, or perhaps a volunteer newly arrived from the 'old states'. Whatever his background, his attire contrasts with that of the other figures. The frock coat, cravat, and waistcoat were *de rigueur* for all 'gentlemen'. His tall hat could be made of silk, but beaver was more common. Most old-time Texians liked to chew their tobacco, but this man prefers to smoke his in a clay pipe; he keeps the easily broken pipe out of harm's way by securing it in his hatband. The sash around his waist provides a cavalier flair, but also serves to secure a flintlock pistol. Like Maj. Williamson he prefers a shotgun, in this case a civilian fowling piece. Indeed, his heavy riding boots are the only concession to the frontier. The silver Mexican spurs would have been bought, or perhaps captured, after coming to Texas.

B: The Battle of Plum Creek, 1840

Background figures depict not only the wide range of

Bonnie Parker and Clyde Barrow, c.1933: clowning for the camera, Bonnie brandishes one of her favoured weapons, a *sawn-off 12-gauge shotgun. (Author's collection; courtesy of Michael Parrish)*

Captain Frank Hamer, c.1934: the nemesis of Bonnie and Clyde. *(Author's collection; courtesy of Michael Parrish)*

civilian apparel worn by rangers, but also the myriad styles of Comanche dress.

B1: Comanche Warrior
The main Comanche figure is the warrior described by Reverend Z. N. Morrell. The brave has adorned his stolen finery with several special Indian touches. He draws attention to an old battle scar by ringing it with war paint, and is armed with a distinctive war club called the *tekniwup*.

B2: Texas Ranger
The main ranger figure portrays an American resident of San Antonio de Béxar. The ensemble of this cocksure gentleman clearly reveals the influence of *tejano* fashion, which includes elaborately embroidered Mexican jacket, spike-rowelled spurs, and a *vaquero* saddle. At the same time he jealously retains

his southern planter's hat, buckskin trousers, and Wellington boots. Weapons consist of a double-barrelled percussion shotgun and a brace of flintlock pistols.

C: Los Diablos Tejanos, 1847
C1: Captain Ben McCulloch
A period lithograph shows McCulloch in a wide-brimmed hat, floppy cravat, white wide-collar shirt, waistcoat, and day jacket. He stuffs his trousers into heavy top-boots, which he also used as a convenient haven for his Bowie knife. Like many early Texians, he has adopted the huge Mexican spurs. The captain has holstered his five-shot Colt Patterson revolver.

C2: Ranger Sergeant
Like his captain, the sergeant is dressed in a fairly orthodox fashion, complete with white shirt, cravat, and wide-collared coat. His only symbols of rank are a

Taken during the late 1940s, this image exemplifies the co-existence of old traditions and new technologies. The helicopter pilot identifies the location of stolen cattle, but the ranger still finds that some jobs are best performed from horseback. (Texas State Library, Archives Division, Austin)

military cloth cap and the sash around his waist. He sports garish checkered overalls typical of the period; note the tight, narrow cut, and the strap attached under the instep. His weapons are a Patterson Colt revolver and flintlock pistols. He is depicted here menacingly testing the edge of his massive Bowie knife.

C3: Ranger Lieutenant

This figure represents a Southern planter type. He also wears checkered trousers, but in a more subtle pattern than C2. An obligatory waistcoat is worn, but note the low cut of this one. Our man, in a somewhat threatening fashion, is cleaning his Colt Patterson revolver; observe that the Patterson's trigger retracts until the hammer has been drawn to the cocked position.

C4: Mexican Peon

The *peon*—a common labourer—wears white muslin, an inexpensive loose cotton fabric. Pants were cut to be tight at the thigh but wider near the ankle; the

plain pull-over shirt has wide sleeves; and a brightly-coloured sash secures the pants. Crude rawhide sandals protect his feet.

D: Hays's Rangers, 1848
D1: Colonel John C. 'Jack' Hays

Mexican War veteran Albert G. Brackett left us a splendid description of Hays as he appeared in Mexico: 'He was very plainly dressed, and wore a blue roundabout, black leather cap, and black pants, and had nothing about him to denote that he belonged to the army, or held military rank in it. His face was sun-browned; his cheeks gaunt, and his dark hair and dark eyes gave a shade of melancholy to his features; he wore no beard or moustache; and his small size—he being about five feet eight—made him appear more like a boy than a man.'

The roundabout was a military jacket, but was often adapted for civilian wear. The lone star insignia is attached to the front of the leather cap. He is mounted astride a Mexican saddle which, along with his spiked spurs, denotes an element of cultural borrowing from his *tejano* neighbours. Many US regulars were astounded by the firepower of the Texas Rangers, most of whom were absolutely festooned with a diverse assortment of weaponry, and Hays was no exception. In his belt he sticks a brace of flintlock pistols, and holstered on the belt are two of the enormous Walker Colt revolvers. He fastens the ubiquitous Bowie knife on his right hip and slings his long rifle across the saddle horn.

D2: Mexican Guerrillero
Like that of the rangers, the attire of the *guerrillero* was a matter of individual taste. This unlucky irregular wears colourful *ranchero* clothing. His tooled leather leggings are called *gamuzas*. *Guerrilleros* attempted to inspire terror with a wide assortment of macabre trappings; the death's-head device on the black lance pennon is based on surviving examples and would have been typical.

D3: Texas Ranger Private
'Rip' Ford wrote of several 'little affairs' on the road from Orizaba to Veracruz, and recalled that 'in one of

these a Mexican officer, said to be a general, was killed. His uniform and chapeau were donned by a ranger'. This figure wears the hat and uniform coat of a Mexican general of brigade. It is exceedingly unlikely, however, that he would have adopted the entire uniform, and the rest of his ensemble appears in stark contrast to the captured regalia. Obviously fond of Mexican fashions, this ranger has 'borrowed' a pair of white muslin pants and the colourful overalls typical of those worn by *vaqueros* in the Veracruz area. The ankle boots have a type of patent spurs that screwed directly into the wooden heel. This ranger carries a Walker Colt and has a Bowie knife on his belt, and has unquestionably succeeded in his efforts 'to dress as outlandishly as possible'.

D4: Tortillera
The clothing of the *tortillera* is more practical than provocative. Making *tortillas* was sweaty, back-breaking work and was normally relegated to servants or street vendors. Ignoring the shocked glances of American invaders, Mexicans deemed it perfectly natural that a woman engaged in such a task would open her blouse to catch the air. The stone slab upon which she pounds unleavened cornmeal is a *metate*. Mexican women often covered their heads with an ornately embroidered shawl called a *reboso*. It is unlikely, however, that the *tortillera* would continue to wear the *reboso* at the same time hot work compelled her to lower her blouse.

E: Canadian River Campaign, 1858
E1: Captain John S. 'Rip' Ford
Ford wears a wide-brimmed hat adorned with the lone star insignia, a morning coat, and striped trousers tucked into heavy top-boots. Large Mexican spurs complete the outfit. He is armed with a Colt First Model Dragoon revolver.

E2: Iron Jacket
Iron Jacket is often incorrectly depicted wearing plate armour. In fact he wore vestiges of a Spanish coat of mail, but by 1858 there was reportedly little of it remaining. He probably wore the armour more for

In 1948 Ranger Dub Naylor donned a diving suit to search for a body in a   *Texas lake. (Texas State Library, Archives Division, Austin)*

its 'medicine' than the protection it provided. He wields a Comanche war horn, after the one housed in the Texas Memorial Museum. The war whistle that hangs about his neck was used to give signals during battle.

E3: Ranger Private
This figure wears a pleated shirt and *vaquero*-style trousers reinforced by a leather section. His firearms are a Colt Second Model .44 Dragoon (Model 1848) and a shotgun.

F: Frontier Defence, 1864
F1: Ranger Captain
This frontier veteran dresses formally in black frock coat, trousers, and waistcoat. The Palmetto hat is reminiscent of those worn by Southern planters, and was far more comfortable during hot Texas summers than those made of beaver or felt. He wears a Mexican blanket draped across his shoulders, a style affected by many old-timers. Sentimentality and stubbornness compel him to retain the old-fashioned Walker Colt revolver that he has used since the Mexican–American War.

F2: Ranger Private
Details are drawn from a period photograph of Dr. Rufus C. Burleson's ranging company. The linsey shirt and trousers would have been representative of those worn by farm boys across the state. His tall riding boots, however, show him to be a horseman—a western 'cowboy', not an eastern 'plowboy'. Most weapons left Texas with state troops serving in

Texas Rangers like to be prepared. This photograph, taken in 1950, displays equipment removed from Ranger John Wood's patrol car when he was issued a new one. (Texas State Library, Archives Division, Austin)

eastern theatres; frontier defenders received what little remained. In this case, the teenager carries an antiquated percussion shotgun that is probably older than he is.

F3: Ranger Sergeant

The vestiges of his Confederate service are the shell jacket, which is homespun butternut rather than regulation grey, and worn laced brogans. The brim of his slouch hat is turned up to better display the lone star insignia. He does not carry a sidearm, as it would be difficult for a one-armed man to load; instead he favours a sawn-off double-barrelled shotgun, devastating at short range.

G: Frontier Battalion, c.1880
G1: Major John B. Jones

Jones is wearing the typical bib-front 'fireman's shirt' with neckerchief. Firearms are the Colt .45 revolver and the round-barrel carbine version of the Winchester 'Yellow Boy'. The major established a reputation as a meticulous dresser, even in the field.

G2: Ranger Private

This man wears a wide-brimmed hat, white shirt, vest, and gaudy checkered trousers over boot tops. He is armed with a later type 'Wesson' shotgun, and carries ammunition in the haversack slung over his shoulder. Repudiating the stereotype, this ranger does not carry a six-shooter.

G3: Ranger Private

This long-haired fellow wears a short jacket unbuttoned, and packs a Model 1874 Sharps Sporter with a 30 in. barrel.

H: McNelly's Rangers, 1876
H1: Captain Leander H. McNelly

Sombre in appearance and demeanour, McNelly dresses formally in dress coat, vest, and neck-tie. His striped trousers are of a type which enjoyed wide popularity in the 1870s. Weapons are a Colt revolver and a Sharps rifle.

H2: Ranger Sergeant

Contrasting with McNelly's decorous ensemble, the sergeant wears garb more typical of the average 1870s ranger. His attire marks him as a horseman; the high-topped boots are equipped with a riding heel, his hands are protected from reins by heavy leather gauntlets, and a bandanna around his neck can quickly cover his mouth and nose from choking dust. Note the stars on the gauntlets and boots; the lone star symbol was affected not only by rangers, but by proud Texans in all walks of life, and by the 1870s there was something approaching a cult of the lone star in Texas fashion.

H3: Ranger Private

The apparel of the youthful private does not notably

Ranger E. J. Banks, 1951, in the typical khaki attire of the 1950s ranger. (Texas State Library, Archives Division, Austin)

Rangers breakfast on black coffee before beginning a horseback patrol of the rugged West Texas countryside sometime in the late 1950s. (Texas State Library, Archives Division, Austin)

differ from that worn by most Texas cowboys of the period. Note the elaborate embroidery (probably hand-stitched by his sweetheart) that decorates the bib of his 'fireman's shirt' and the galaxy of stars that adorn his outfit. This young man is left-handed, thus the cross-draw position of his holstered Colt revolver.

H4: Nueces Strip outlaw

This melancholy felon wears a distinctive Mexican jacket that extends only to mid-waist. The short jackets, which were produced in a wide assortment of bright colours, seem always to have been worn over a white shirt. His *vaquero* trousers are shielded by the richly tooled leather *gamuzas*. He enjoys a last smoke while sitting astride the pilfered Dick Heye saddle that has been his undoing.

I: Texas Rangers, 1915–1930
I1: Border Ranger, 1915

This figure is drawn from a photograph of a ranger taken in Río Grande City, Texas. By the turn of the century many rangers had rejected the historic Colt revolver for the Colt .45 automatic, as here. His rifle is the Model 1895 Winchester carbine, which had proved effective during the Spanish–American War

and when employed by civilian hunters; produced until 1938, this box-magazine repeater was widely sold abroad. Still distinctly Texan, this man's twill shirt and khaki trousers present a more modern appearance than the traditional cowboy attire.

I2: Captain Jerry Gray, 1921

Details are from a photograph in the Barker Texas History Center at the University of Texas. Like many of his predecessors who had served along the Mexican border, Gray reveals a taste for Hispanic fashions. Note the straw sombrero, the double-row cartridge belt, and the elaborate stitching on the uppers of his 'stovepipe' boots, which have snout-nosed toes and thick soles.

I3: Ranger C. L. 'Blackie' Blackwell, 1921

The figure was drawn after a photograph taken at Presidio, Texas, which portrays Blackwell as he appeared while serving with Capt. Gray. 'Blackie' has adopted several Mexican accoutrements including an imposing sombrero, bandolier, and oversized bandanna. He packs two Colt revolvers and the Model 1895 Winchester carbine.

J: Texas Ranger Captains, 1930–1950
J1: Adjutant General William Warren Sterling, c.1930

Born on the family ranch in 1891, young Sterling was the living image of a Texas cowboy. By the time he became adjutant general, however, neckties and three-piece suits constituted his everyday dress. Even so, vestiges of his brush country upbringing remain; note the wide-brimmed Stetson hat, the massive buckle and belt, and, of course, his cowboy boots. Broad-shouldered, rugged and tall, Sterling once served as the model for a Texas Ranger statue.

J2: Captain Francis Augustus Hamer, c.1932

Born in 1884, Hamer grew up in West Texas and in his youth hired out as a wrangler. Because he knew and had been the genuine article, Hamer despised those 'drugstore cowboys' who wore range gear only to awe city slickers; consequently, Frank—few called him Francis more than once—refused to wear boots and riding outfit unless he was actually in the saddle. Photographs taken after he killed Clyde Barrow and Bonnie Parker show him attired as a typical 1930s businessman, in suit and tie. Here he is shown inspecting Parker's sawn-off shotgun, one of 15 firearms removed from the outlaws' car following the fatal ambush.

J3: Captain Manuel T. 'Lone Wolf' Gonzaullas, c.1950

Reported to have been the 'niftiest dresser in the Ranger Service', Gonzaullas is shown as he appeared near the end of his career. Period photographs show

Captain M. T. 'Lone Wolf' Gonzaullas, whose 'trotline' tamed oil-boom towns in the 1920s, as he appeared toward the end of his career. (Texas State Library, Archives Division, Austin)

'Lone Wolf' wearing an all-khaki outfit, a white Stetson, and polished black Wellington boots. An avid weapon collector, Gonzaullas is depicted packing ornamented twin Colt .45 revolvers; these were 'dress' pistols and were not typical of the plain ones he normally carried in the field.

K: Modern Texas Rangers, 1970–1990
K1: Ranger Aubrey D. Bryce

Attire consists of a white cowboy hat, white dress shirt, black tie, tan gabardine trousers, and polished black cowboy boots. The ranger badge is worn over the left breast. Note the tie tack in the form of the ranger badge. During the hot summer months he would probably opt for a short-sleeve white shirt.

K2: Ranger Ron Stewart

Stewart wears a straw cowboy hat, white dress shirt, black tie, a leather vest, western-cut twill trousers, and cowboy boots. The badge is worn on the vest—as always, on the left breast. His belt buckle is a variation on the state seal; Texans still display a distinct fondness for their lone star insignia.

K3: Captain Jack Dean

The captain is shown here in the only 'semi-official' apparel the Texas Rangers ever had, the tan gabardine suit, 'worn mainly for funerals and photographs'. The suit was always worn with a white cowboy hat, black tie, and polished cowboy boots. Capt. Dean, however, reports that this formal dress was discontinued in the mid-1970s. Now, as in the old days, Texas Rangers dress as they please.

Captain Clint Peoples. After eleven years as a DPS patrolman, Peoples became a Texas Ranger in 1946. He made captain seven years later, and in 1969 became senior ranger captain. (Texas State Library, Archives Division, Austin)

INDEX

(References to illustrations are shown in **bold**. Plates are shown with caption locators in brackets)

Alamo 6, 13
Aldrich, Capt. R.W. **52**
Armstrong, First Sgt. John B. 29, 32, 45
Austin, Stephen Fuller **3**, 3, **4**, 4

Banks, Ranger E.J. **60**
Bass, Sam **28**, 28
Bird, Capt. John 6–7
Blackwell, C.L. 'Blackie': **I3** (61)
Bonnie & Clyde 50–1, **56**, 62
Bowie knives 20, **C1** (56), **D1** (58), **D3** (58)
Brooks, Capt. J.A. 46, **55**
Brown, Maj. Jacob 15
Bryce, Ranger Aubrey D.: **K1** (63)

Callahan, James H. 21–2
Cameron, Capt. Ewen 14–15
Canales purge 48, 49
cattle rustling 26, 27, 30, 32, 46
Cortina, Juan Nepomuceno **20**, 22–3, 29
Crowder, Capt. R.A. 'Bob' 52

Dean, Capt. Jack: **K3** (63)

feuds 26–7, 29, 32
firearms 54, **59**, 59–60, **62**
  ammunition 5, **31**, **53**, **G2** (60), **I2/3** (61)
  Colt revolvers 12, 13, 19, **H1** (60), **H3**(61), **I3** (61)
    .45s: **G1** (60), **J3** (63)
    Dragoons: **E1** (58), **E3** (59)
    Pattersons **10**, 12, 19, **C1/2/3** (56, 57)
    Walkers 19–20, **D1/3** (58), **E1** (59)
  flintlock pistols **4**, **5**, **B2** (56), **C2** (57), **D1** (58)
  long rifles 11–12, **A2** (55), **D1** (58)
  Sharps 30, **G3** (60), **H1** (60)
  Shotguns **56**, 62, **A1/3** (55), **B2** (56), **E3** (59), **F2/3** (60), **G2** (60)
  Winchesters **31**, **G1** (60), **I1/3** (61)
Ford, Capt. John Salmon **16**, 19–20, 21, 22, 23, 58, **E1** (58)

Gault, Ranger B.M. 'Manny' 50–1
Gildea, Ranger A.M. **27**
Gillett, James S. 21
Gonzaullas, Capt. Manuel T. 50, 52, **62**, **J3** (62–3)
Gray, Capt. Jerry **54**, **I2** (61)

Hall, Lt. Lee 31–2
Hall, Ranger Robert **23**
Hamer, Capt. Francis Augustus 50–1, 52, **55**, **56**, **J2** (62)
Hardin, John Wesley **32**, 32–45
Hays, Col. John C. **8**, 10–13, 15, 16, 17, 19, 20, 21, 31, **D1** (57–8)
horse-stealing 3, 4, 7, 8, 16, 46
Howard, Judge Charles H. 27–8
Hughes, Capt. John R. **46**, 46, **47**, **55**
Huston, Gen. Felix 9, 10

Indian tribes 3, 4, 11, **19**, 21, 22, 24
  Comanches 3, 6-13, 20, **21**, 22, 24, 25, **B** (55–6), **E2** (58–9)
  Tonkawas 4, 10, **19**, 22
intelligence gathering **11**, **12**, 15, 16–17, 18, 32, 52
Iron Jacket 22, **E2** (58–9)

Johnson, Ranger Charles August **32**
Jones, Maj. John B. **24**, 25–7, 28, 29, 46, **G1** (60)

labour disputes **47**, 49, 53

McCulloch, Capt. Ben 9, **12**, 14, 18, 20, 24, **C1** (56)
McDonald, Capt. W.J. 'Bill' 46–7, **49**
Mackenzie, Col. Ranald S. 24
McNelly, Capt. Leander H. **29**, 29–32, **H1** (60)
Mexico 3, 4, 5–6, **7**, 20, 47
  Mexican-American War **13**, 13–20, **14**, **15**, **C** (56–7), **D** (57–8)
  border activity 21–2, 22–3, 29–32, 46, 47–9, **H** (60–1), **I** (61)
Moore, Col. John 10
Murry, Capt. Sam **31**

Naylor, Ranger Dub 58
Nueces 7, 15, **26**, 29–30, **H4** (61)

Oglethorpe, Gen. James Edward 4
Outlaws **28**, 28, 29, 30, **32**, 32–45, 46, 50–1, **56**, **H4** (61)

Peoples, Capt. Clint **63**
Placido, Chief **19**, 22
Plum Creek 10, **19**, **B** (55–6)
Prohibition 48–9, 50
publicity **14**, 15–16, **21**, **22**, **26**, 52

Ranger attire 4, 8, 13, 19, 46
  Illustrations **16**, **18**, **23**, **27**, **31**, **53**, **60**, **A–K** (54–63)
  insignia **14**, 46, 57, 58, 60, 63
Ranger formations 4–6, **7**, 18, 21, 26, 46, 49, 51–4
  Canadian River campaign 21, 22, **E** (58–9)
  Dept of Public Safety 51–2, 53
  frontier defence: **F** (59–60)
    Frontier Battalion 24–8, **32**, 45, 46, 46, **47**, 48, **G** (60)
  los Diablos Tejanos 13–20, **C** (56–7), **D** (57–8)
  McNelly's 29–32, **H** (60–1)
  Williamson's 5–6, **A** (54–5)
Ranger resources 4, 5, 8, 13, **25**, 51
  automobiles 49, **53**, 53, 54, **59**
  investigative aids 52, **57**, 58
  modern equipment 54, **59**, **62**
Rangers: **B2** (56), **I1/3** (61), **K1/2** (63)
  Majors 5, **A1** (54–5), **G1** (60)
  captains 4, 5, 8, 46, **C1** (56), **E1** (58), **F1** (59), **H1** (60), **I2** (61), **J** (62–3), **K3** (63)
  lieutenants 5, **C3** (57)
  sergeants 31, **C2** (56–7), **F3** (60), **H2** (60)
  privates 5, **A2/3** (55), **D3** (58), **E3** (59), **F2** (59–60), **G2/3** (60), **H3** (60–1)
Roberts, Capt. Dan W. 25, **55**

Saddles 5, 13, 18, 29, **B2** (56), **D1** (57), **H4** (61)
Santa Anna, Antonio L. de 5, 6, 14, 18
Schmitt, Capt. G.H. **47**
Scott, Gen. Winfield 17–18, 19, 20
Sterling, Adjt Gen. William Warren 50, **55**, **J1** (62)
Stewart, Ranger Ron: **K2** (63)
Sullivan, Ranger Sgt. W.J.L. **31**

Taylor, Gen. Zachary 13–18
Tays, Lt. John B. 27–8
tejanos 3, **7**, 13, **14**, 29, 48, 49, **B2** (56), **D1** (57–8)
Tumlinson, Capt. John J. 5, 6, 9

Walker, Samuel Hamilton **11**, 15, 19, 20
Wallace, Capt. William 'Bigfoot' 15, **17**, 21, 54
Williamson, Maj. Robert McAlpin 5, **6**, 6, 11, **A1** (54–5)

COMPANION SERIES FROM OSPREY

MEN-AT-ARMS
An unrivalled source of information on the organisation, uniforms and equipment of the world's fighting men, past and present. The series covers hundreds of subjects spanning 5,000 years of history. Each 48-page book includes concise texts packed with specific information, some 40 photos, maps and diagrams, and eight colour plates of uniformed figures.

WARRIOR
Definitive analysis of the appearance, weapons, equipment, tactics, character and conditions of service of the individual fighting man throughout history. Each 64-page book includes full-colour uniform studies in close detail, and sectional artwork of the soldier's equipment.

ORDER OF BATTLE
The most detailed information ever published on the units which fought history's great battles. Each 96-page book contains comprehensive organisation diagrams supported by ultra-detailed colour maps. Each title also includes a large fold-out base map.

CAMPAIGN
Concise, authoritative accounts of history's decisive military encounters. Each 96-page book contains over 90 illustrations including maps, orders of battle, colour plates, and three-dimensional battle maps.

NEW VANGUARD
Comprehensive histories of the design, development and operational use of the world's armoured vehicles and artillery. Each 48-page book contains eight pages of full-colour artwork including a detailed cutaway.

AIRCRAFT OF THE ACES
Focuses exclusively on the elite pilots of major air campaigns, and includes unique interviews with surviving aces sourced specifically for each volume. Each 96-page volume contains up to 40 specially commissioned artworks, unit listings, new scale plans and the best archival photography available.

COMBAT AIRCRAFT
Technical information from the world's leading aviation writers on the century's most significant military aircraft. Each 96-page volume contains up to 40 specially commissioned artworks, unit listings, new scale plans and the best archival photography available.